Writer's Insights – Tips for Ultimate Success

By Suzie Carr

Cover art by Germz Designs (www.germz808.com)

Also by Suzie Carr:
The Fiche Room
Tangerine Twist
Two Feet off The Ground
Inner Secrets
A New Leash on Life
The Muse
Staying True
Snowflakes
The Journey Somewhere
Sandcastles

Keep up on Suzie's latest news and projects:
www.curveswelcome.com

Follow Suzie on Twitter:
@girl_novelist

For you, My Sunshine.

Contents

FORWARD

I've been fascinated with writing novels since high school, but I didn't start to actually write one until many years later. A part of me feared I'd fail miserably at the one thing I wanted to do more than anything in this world. Talk about dumping a ton of pressure on oneself! Instead of writing, I spent my weekends absorbing the pages of countless how-to books in my local Books-A-Million café. I'd sit quietly, steaming mug of flavored coffee on one side and a pile of books on the other, intent on learning everything I could about how to write a novel.

That particular bookstore had an entire bookshelf dedicated to such an adventure; I believe I read most every one of them. As I studied, my interest and intrigue into novel writing outgrew my fears.

I finally tiptoed into professional writing by submitting an article to a spa management magazine on how to conduct a team meeting – a topic about which I felt confident writing. I submitted it with crossed fingers and toes, hoping the editor would respond kindly! Well, she did. And she did so within an hour of my emailing it to her. I made my first three hundred dollars as a writer!

Seeing my name printed in an international magazine lifted my confidence. The very day I flipped through the pages and saw my article, I committed to writing that novel I'd always had waiting patiently in the back of my mind. I wrote the first three chapters of it, showed it to a few people I trusted, and then let it die when one of them told me he didn't understand the point of my story at all. His brutal honesty cut through me like shrapnel. I put off writing another novel for many years. Then, I met a new friend who enjoyed the same genre of books as me. We talked endlessly about books. As our conversations continued to blossom, so did my imagination. I began talking to her about ideas for a novel, and she encouraged me to get writing.

So, in 2003, I set out to write *The Fiche Room.*

Twelve years later, my passion for writing continues to grow exponentially with each new book I write. In these years, I've had the pleasure of meeting so many wonderful readers and fellow writers, and have learned so much from them.

The most rewarding part for me, in the process of becoming part of the writing community at large, is when people ask me for writing advice. I am always humbled, grateful, and incredibly excited to share with them the things I've learned through the years.

As time progresses, more and more aspiring writers have reached out to me via social media, asking me questions about writing. From these questions, I created my first educational series, *The Writer's Insights Video Series.* From those videos, I received so many more questions, I thought, *hey, I should write a book and address them!*

So here is what I've learned over the years from trial and error, from successful people, from reading lots of books and studying them, and from interacting with a group of wonderful readers and fellow writers whose curiosity into the written word excites and propels me to continue learning as much as I can about the art of creative writing.

- Suzie Carr

Chapter One

3 Essentials to Productive Writing

First of all, if you are picking up this book because you have a burning desire to write a book of your own, then I am thrilled for you! Writing is a beautiful art form where the writer can capture her deepest loves, fears, vulnerabilities, insights, and creative ideas, then share them with others in a way that is entertaining, educational, and life-affirming.

Writing a book offers a person a sense of empowerment and purpose that can inform, inspire, and play with emotions. By getting thoughts down on paper, a person frees herself to explore the world from different lenses and angles.

Tapping into the mind of a character and discovering new ways of dealing with conflict is the greatest mind-blowing gift a writer will likely experience. Through our characters, we can empathize, grow, and develop a new perspective on life, and share that newly gained knowledge with others.

Writers who can let their minds go and travel into the psyche of characters are ones who will write prose that will capture the hearts and

1

minds of readers, captivating them in a state of awe well past the last page of their stories.

To accomplish this great feat, writers must feel more deeply, open their minds to discovery, and disregard self-judgment.

Once committed to the creative and emotional journey, writers can benefit from creating a set of ground rules that will keep them focused, organized, and spot-on as they tell their story.

I can't think of a better way to enjoy life than through the written word. If you feel the same, then let's get started.

Let's discuss the three essential elements to productive writing.

STEP 1: MAKE TIME TO WRITE

Carving out time for writing is one of the most difficult parts of being a writer. Life is busy. We may have children and pets in need of our attention. We often have full-time jobs that require our focus, time, and dedication. We have floors that need to be vacuumed, toilets to be cleaned, and counters to be scrubbed. We have breakfasts, lunches and dinners to prep. We have relationships to nurture. Then of course we have Facebook, Twitter, Pinterest, and Instagram to keep up with, too. The list is endless.

What to do?

If we want to be writers, then we must write. It is the only way to become and remain one.

Be Productive or the Dream Dies

To be productive, you must enjoy the process of taking action on your writing goals. If you're not enjoying it, you may need to re-evaluate your goals and make sure they are truly what you want to achieve. Writing a book takes tremendous focus, energy, and time. A burning desire to write is a must and will carry you through those tough moments many writers face.

That being said, creating goals is just one part of the process of moving forward. Once you've written down those goals in a place you will see them daily (and you should make them extremely visible), you need to take action on them. DAILY!

Where most people fail to accomplish goals is in the execution of them. Why? Many reasons stand as obstacles, but perhaps one of the biggest is time.

If we analyze our time, we will probably conclude that we waste a lot of it. How many hours of television do you watch? How many times a day do you scroll through your Facebook or Twitter feeds? While these activities are beneficial when done in moderation because they can help us wind down and connect with others, too much can steal valuable productive time.

There's a delicate balance.

Don't Wait to be Inspired

A common mistake that will derail any aspiring writer in her tracks is believing she must wait to write until inspiration strikes.

A famous painter, Thomas Kincaid, once spoke about inspiration. He never waited for it to strike because to do so would put him in a place of creative disadvantage.

He felt that instead of waiting for inspiration to strike, an artist should place himself in the path of inspiration by committing to daily action. Sit in that chair. Place your fingers on that keyboard. Fill that blank screen. If you wait for a slice of time to open itself up for you, you may never move again. You must carve it out and dedicate yourself to filling it with writing.

Fit Writing into Your Busy Life

Decide why you are writing

What is the driving force? What is going to get you up out of bed at an early hour or keep you awake late into the night? What will help you turn off the television, take time away from your loved ones, and shed all your vulnerabilities on the blank screen?

When you know the *why* behind your dreams, and it's a strong *why*, nothing will stand in your way. That reality television show will not become a distraction. That happy hour with friends will not rob you of that next scene planting in your creative mind. That snooze button will not win out over your characters' stories.

Schedule your writing just as you would schedule an appointment

Some writers have told me they take a calendar and jot down their writing appointments. If you're the type that wouldn't dare miss an appointment with a doctor, hairdresser, or business client, then this technique will likely prove successful. I do this. I use a traditional wall calendar, post my writing schedule on it, and check off each day as I progress. This process keeps me on track by holding me accountable. And, I must say, the geek in me loves the act of checking the task off at the end of a writing session.

Stop dreaming about how much you want to write

Getting stuck in the talk of writing is completely natural. We want everyone to know what we're doing. We want them to get equally excited about the characters and storylines we've dreamed up. We love seeing their reactions as we talk about the conflicts that will pop up on the pages of the novel we will write. Talking up an idea has its value, especially if we speak with avid readers who know a good storyline when they see or hear one. The danger comes in when we spend too much time seeking feedback on our ideas even when we know that in order to lift it off the ground, we must get started on it.

Schedule television and internet time

By scheduling, you'll be less apt to mindlessly scroll through the channels or social media newsfeeds and more apt to make strategic decisions. Think of your time as a valuable asset. How do you want to tap into it? How can you best preserve it for effective use?

Write down your top goals

Take some time to flesh out writing goals. Write them down somewhere you will see them. Make it a point to read the goals. Take earnest action on them daily.

Quantify your goals so you can adequately measure them. Some writers like to commit to a daily word, scene, or time count. Figure out which one resonates with you, and make it happen.

Commit at the very least to 15 minutes a day to taking action on one or more of your goals. By taking action daily, you are chunking these massive goals down into digestible steps. Those steps add up over time, and before long, you'll look back on them and realize how far you've come. Action steps also create momentum, which will fuel your desire to continue taking more steps.

Breathe

When you are feeling unfocused, stop what you are doing, go someplace quiet, close your eyes, and breathe. If your mind wanders, focus on counting to four as you inhale and again as you exhale. Listen to your breaths and feel the energy move in and out of you. As simplistic as this sounds, it is the best way to reenergize when in a pinch. Breathe deeply for three minutes, and you'll feel your energy and focus return.

Treat yourself

Rewarding yourself for accomplishing a milestone can help build and sustain motivation over the long haul. Create milestones for your goals, and when reached, gift yourself with something affirming that will perk you up and keep you going until you reach the next one.

STEP 2: GET CREATIVE JUICES FLOWING

For some writers, getting the juices to flow is easy. For others, just thinking the words *I must be creative* stops all color, ideas, and creative flow.

Don't Give Up

Interestingly enough, the day I sat down to write this section, my creativity waned. I sat in front of my blank computer screen and fiddled with Facebook for a while. When I grew bored there, I hopped onto Twitter and followed up on a few tweets and direct messages. Finally, I clicked back into Word and faced the blank screen, upset with myself for wasting valuable writing time on activities that didn't get my fingers moving against the keys.

Why do we, as writers, go into these mind-numbing periods when nothing seems to flow into the creative parts of our brain? For me, I think it's panic that I've reached my cerebral capacity in life. I start to go down that mental path where I ask myself silly questions like, *what if no more ideas ever come to fruition* and *will anyone really want to read what I've written?*

I'd be shocked if I discovered one writer in this world who could tell me honestly that this creative void has never happened to her before.

It happens. It happens to all of us. However, a moment of restless activity in the brain does not equate to the end of your creative road.

Here's What is Really Happening

Creativity is elusive. It can appear and disappear just as quickly. The more we push ourselves to be creative, the more apt we are to lose touch with it. Creativity cannot be forced. In fact, forcing it will only repel. *But*, you might be thinking, *I'm a writer, and I need to stay productive! I can't afford to sit idle!*

I agree. Writers need to stay productive. Writers write, after all. If we aren't writing, we aren't producing, and we aren't moving further along our creative paths.

Stay Productive

The secret to staying productive as a writer is to discover how to switch that light on and off at your will. Remove the fear of losing your creative touch and you'll free yourself. When you're free, you allow the magic to unfold.

My secret to squashing the fear and staying productive is to tap into my creative muse.

You might be thinking, *but, I don't have a muse!*

Everyone has a muse. Many just don't realize it.

A creative muse can be found in everything. It's in a sunset, in a star, in a bird's chirp, and in the melody of a beautiful song. A muse is that special thing that can stop us in our tracks, can hang our jaws in awe, can tune out the rest of the world when it's in our presence, and can lift us to a more fruitful level of being.

The greatest part about this is that every person has access to this inner muse.

Find Your Muse

The trick to finding yours is tapping into your senses and letting them fly freely. Once you set your senses free, you enter a zone where you can create a world that touches and inspires others.

To tap into yours, you must clear your mind.

Unlock Your Creativity

I challenge you to experiment with the following actions to see which one most effectively gets you into that creative zone. Perhaps all of them will or maybe just one is the key to unlocking your creative door.

Sit quietly and listen to music

Really listen to the beats, the melody, and the lyrics. Focus solely on the song. Block out all other distractions and go inward. Breathe deeply. Let the air flow in and relax you.

Create a visual stimulant

Create a collage of colors, shapes, and words, then stare at it through unfocused eyes. Allow your mind to wander into the shapes, ignoring the world around you. By playing with abstract visuals, you can filter out the noise of reason and cultivate a beneficial oasis for new thoughts.

Move

Get up and move for ten minutes. Break out into a light jog, brisk walk, or jumping jacks – whatever you can safely perform.

Jumpstarting your heart in this way will get your mind off any rigidity. You'll focus on something other than your inability to be creative. That's the trick with all of these, you see… to get your mind off the obvious, and get it focused outside that bubble of unproductive thought.

Read quotes

Quotes are a great way to interrupt routine thoughts. They can help you carve out new ways of looking at the world and get you thinking on a higher level outside yourself and onto the frequency of the unexplored world around you.

Meditate or pray

Deep breathing, positive affirmations, and reaching out to a higher power may help you disengage from negative vibes that can steal your joy and inner child. One of the most powerful actions you can take to rid yourself of deflating thoughts is to change your frequency. Meditating and praying can certainly help with that!

Visit with nature

Sit on a park bench. Stare up at a tree. Admire a flower.

Nature has an incredible ability to center and balance a person. When breathing in fresh air and enjoying the majesty of Mother Nature, you'll open yourself to see how beautiful and magical life is. Tapping into this awesomeness can lift you to new perspectives.

When you change your view, you allow yourself to interpret the world in a new light. Whenever you take the focus off an old way of thinking and place it on a new vantage point, you free yourself to experience a whole new world that you may have otherwise missed.

Play with color

Get a paint brush and splash paint on a canvas or color on paper with a crayon.

Sometimes the worst thing we can do as writers is sit in front of a computer and will creativity to take up root. Some of my most creative moments are when I'm away from the computer and doing a different creative activity. I'm an oil painter, too, and when I'm feeling stumped, I get out my canvas, paints, and brushes, and start splashing color on it. I block everything else out, and just give in to the rush of turning a blank canvas into color. Freewriting, which I'll get into in a moment, and painting are my staples for revving up my writing mind.

Join a book club

Joining a book club is one of the most effective ways to understand what readers really desire and expect from a novelist.

To be a better writer, read more. Writers have doled out this advice to aspiring novelists for a long time. A well-read writer is better equipped to transform thoughts into meaningful stories. The more a writer reads, the more she will understand the subtle nuances that get readers turning pages.

By reading from a variety of genres, you'll gain a three-dimensional perspective on what is most important in a book. Some of the greatest benefits and writing lessons I've learned have come directly from my book club meetings.

You'll read the good and the bad. Everyone has a different opinion on what creates that urge to flip to the next page when the eyes are tired but curiosity demands full-steam ahead. You'll be exposed to books that will take you on journeys you never imagined traveling. You'll read outside your comfort zone and reach higher into the nebulous world of fantasy, the intoxicating rush of a heated romance, and turn onto the fast-lane of action. Traveling on these literary pathways will widen your perspective and grant you a front-row seat to whole new experiences.

We've all probably said at one point, *gosh I'd love to be a fly on the wall right about now.* Well, as a writer, no greater gift to insight exists than that of gaining access to the inner workings of the reader's mind as she pours over words crafted by a fellow novelist. To understand what readers think about characters, motives, themes, and plots is to understand what makes a great book a great book. What better clarity can a writer experience?

A book club places you center stage in front of your readers. The view is truly spectacular and eye-opening.

Freewrite for ten minutes

Freewriting puts writers in a magical place where they set themselves free to explore fantasy, reality, and everything in between. Set a timer and write without any regard for grammar, spelling, or logic. Just write whatever pops into your mind and don't stop to analyze or think. This exercise can set you up for a productive writing session.

Start typing and don't stop. Write about the first thing your eyes land upon. If it's your desk, write about how it feels, looks, or smells. If your mind wanders to another object, let it. Allow your mind to write about the most random thoughts and patterns. Just keep typing! Let your senses go wild.

The benefits of free writing are numerous. It allows you to clear your mind of clutter and to purposely break the rules. By doing so, characters come alive and let their voices be heard. Narrative voice comes out of hiding and ideas flow.

Express yourself without rules

Rules and restrictions limit our creativity. When we fret over whether a verb agrees with its subject or whether a sentence is too passive versus active, we unplug the power of imagination. Writing is all about unleashing what's deep in our mind. When we bind to rules, we suffocate those powerful emotions that bring a string of words to life. Set yourself free by eliminating all judgment until you've gotten the words out where they belong. The only rule to follow when you freewrite is to set a goal of either time (ten minutes is highly recommended) or space (1-2 pages).

Remove anxiety and pressure

When setting out to write a first book, many writers run into major writer's block. They sit and stare at the white space and panic. They try to type a sentence and can't think of a single word. The pressure of filling white space with a saleable story can kill an idea before it even has time to live. To avoid this, temporarily rethink the purpose of this whiteness as a safe place where you can jot down any thought that pops into mind. The goal is to remove all pressure by clearing the mind of clutter, and ultimately getting the words to flow.

Find your voice

Every writer has a style, but many struggle to discover it. When you freewrite you learn to find your unique style. By giving your thoughts the freedom to spill out onto the screen, you are in essence allowing your opinions and true voice to come through. As a writer, when you find your voice, you bring your writing to a whole new level. You'll likely uncover feelings you didn't even know existed.

We're all wired differently. For some, you may find your ideas on a wooded path in the middle of a forest. For others, you might have better luck listening to Baroque classical music while sipping some wine. Still others might only find their muse in the loving arms of their higher power. The concept to remember here is to figure out what works for you and go do it. You've got future readers waiting!

STEP 3: KEEP UP THE MOMENTUM

So, let's say you've found your time. You've got ideas flowing. And, now you're deep into the creative groove. Storyline, characters, and settings are popping into your mind with every breath. You are in the early stages of a writer's high!

You wake from a great night's rest, ready to tackle your next chapter. You rise to a sun-filled room, stretch, sip coffee, slip into your favorite chair to begin, rest your fingers on your keyboard and smile at the rapid beat of your words as they come pouring out of your imagination to build upon your new, intoxicating world.

Then you wake up to reality and stare at your fresh computer screen with panic. Your fingers have nothing to type because your mind is sitting blank behind glossed-over eyes.

Instantly, you fear you've lost your writing mojo. All those ideas that came to you over the weeks that prefaced this new chapter splatter into a heap of nothingness. Where did all the snappy dialogue and plot twists go? Poof. Gone. Just like that, as soon as you sat in front of that blank computer screen.

It happens to all of us.

Here are some ways to get your writing mojo back, should this happen:

Be a fly on the wall

Imagine your lead character is having a conversation with someone she cares deeply about. What would that conversation look like? How would she be reacting? What would be the vibe? Would she be having an argument, indulging in friendly debate, confessing something, or trying to make someone feel better?

Get in your character's head

Imagine your lead character sitting on a comfy chair, glass of wine in one hand, a pen in the other as she writes in her journal. What is she writing about? What happened in her day that made her smile, made her mad, confused her, or enticed her? Is she hard on herself? Or perhaps she's in denial over something?

Make a writing goal

As I mentioned earlier, setting a goal is the first step in achieving measurable results. Some writers have great success creating a daily or weekly word-count goal. Others have more success setting a scene or chapter goal. Find out what works for you, write it down, then follow it. At the end of a week, regroup by analyzing how far you've come.

Indulge your senses

Take a walk, sit in a different room to break out of routine, dance, cook, do something that puts you in a scene in your book. What does the smell remind you of? Is it bright, dark, peaceful or chaotic? If you could taste the setting, how would you describe it? What does the air feel like? Is it exotically moist, delicate, or frenzied?

Use a writing prompt

Open up a magazine, newspaper, or favorite book, and pick a random sentence. Imagine your character is at the tail end of that sentence. What happens next? Using a writing prompt can get you unstuck and out of your writer head and into character mode.

Ask the important question

Stare down your character in your mind and ask her, "What if XYZ happened to you instead?" See where she takes you with her answer. This is a great way to give life to dull scenes and dragging plot lines. Nothing adds a spark like tossing in a curve and seeing how one might react to it. Keep your character guessing, and your readers will be just as hooked to see what happens next.

ONE-ON-ONE – GETTING IT DONE

I sat down with life coach, Eric Williamson, of Tailored Training Solutions (tailoredtrainingsolutions.com) and asked him for his insights on staying focused.

Q. What if a person has too many demands conflicting with his schedule to make room for the pursuit of a dream? What advice would you give?

Eric: When pursuing your dream, it has to be a priority. You may likely face that moment when you stare directly into a deep fear that you may never become the person you dreamed of becoming because of competing desires. At that point, you need to revisit them, rank them accordingly, then make time to work on them. It's as simple and necessary as that.

Planning your life takes serious commitment. One of the greatest fears you may experience is failing to take advantage of your potential. But, if you really want to make it happen, you cannot make excuses or cave into fear.

Through time, your goals and responsibilities may even expand and challenge you to manage competing ones. You may have a baby, a new job, a new marriage, or a new home. You may encounter twists and turns on your road to achievement because that road is seldom formed in a straight line. Sometimes you must take the harder path, and in so doing you may encounter obstacles and hurdles that block you. But, you have to stay focused, remain patient, and stay committed to pursuing your path.

You should also surround yourself with a small group of positive and supportive people. I recommend having an "accountabilibuddy," which is someone who will hold you accountable for achieving tasks. For example, if you plan to write ten pages within a week, your accountabilibuddy will support you by checking in with you to make sure you are on task.

Here is an example of how this concept works. I completed a public speaking workshop about a month ago where I helped young entrepreneurs improve their public speaking. These entrepreneurs were competing with others in a "shark tank" style forum for cash prizes to support their business. During that time, I had the opportunity to hear these young entrepreneurs articulate their goal, vision, and passion for starting a business. Although I helped provide them with the necessary public speaking tools needed to communicate with investors and other professionals, I also gave them positive feedback and encouraged their business goals. This built their confidence and self-esteem, helping them to maintain their focus when they were most challenged with competing priorities.

Q. Why do people procrastinate on something as important as a dream? How can they overcome that?

Eric: People procrastinate for various reasons. Some people procrastinate out of fear of failure. Sometimes you may not truly believe you can achieve it. You may fear failing because it may mean the end of pursuing the dream that's kept your heart pumping with vigor. Also, it could be that the plan for pursuing a dream is unclear. It's difficult to achieve anything without a plan. Dreams are achieved through action. Tasks to help you achieve them should be clearly identified and outlined. When a plan is written down, procrastinating is more difficult and focusing becomes easier. You may also procrastinate because you may not be serious about your pursuits and will look for excuses that inhibit achievement. Be mindful of this so you can course correct and get back on track.

Q. How can a person regain focus on a goal?

Eric: Regaining focus on a goal takes drive, commitment, and perseverance. You can regain focus on a goal when you employ Emotional Intelligence (EQ). One of the key components of EQ is self-awareness. When you are self-aware, you may discover that you have either not invested the time and energy in achieving your goal or that your competing priorities are hindering you from that goal. Once you become self-aware, you can take appropriate steps to regain focus.

You can regain focus on your goal by keeping a journal. Your written commitment will remind you to work on the plan and help you stay accountable. Also, staying connected with supportive people in a positive environment who will hold you accountable and honest about achieving your goal is extremely helpful. Never keep your goal a secret. Tell everyone who will listen. When you constantly talk about it and document it, you will regain focus and it will keep you honest about what you really want to accomplish.

Create a plan. It's very difficult to achieve your goal if you do not understand what it is or what it takes to achieve it. Once you have a plan, and you can clearly understand what you want to accomplish, you can take the necessary steps to recharge and head toward that finish line.

Q. When people face an obstacle, what are some ways to get around it so it doesn't block them from moving forward?

Eric: To continue moving forward from an obstacle, you have to be willing to accept failure. When you fail, you have to learn from the situation and figure out how to approach it differently. Look for the lessons in failure. You have to stay focused, committed, and driven. Employing a high emotional intelligence will help you overcome the obstacle and achieve your goal. For example, reacting calm and poised under pressure can help you stay focused to work toward a solution. Continue to surround yourself with positive and supportive people; they will encourage you to continue despite obstacles. When you face a roadblock, look at it as an opportunity to find solutions. The way you choose to react, learn, and grow in the face of adversity and failure can make you stronger and give you the confidence to continue moving forward despite any obstacle that comes your way.

Q. Is there any other piece of advice you have to offer aspiring writers from a life coaching perspective?

Eric: Embrace adversity, failure, and challenges. Doing this will make it more rewarding and fulfilling when you achieve your goal. It will make you a stronger, wiser, and more grounded person. In order to achieve your goal, don't be afraid to step outside of your comfort zone.

CHAPTER INSIGHTS

- Schedule writing time
- Make a goal and take action on it daily
- Place yourself in the path of inspiration, instead of waiting for it to land in your life
- Discover your muse and remain connected
- Join a book club
- When stuck, freewrite
- Get an "accountabilibuddy" to keep you on track
- View obstacles as opportunities for growth

Chapter Two

Build a Strong Foundation

STEP 1: CREATE A WORKING TITLE

One of the first steps I take before I write a single word of my novel is to create a working title. It keeps me excited as I journey into the new world I'm creating, and also gives the project a sense of realism. With every book I've written, the working title became the ultimate title. Except for this one time... Let me explain.

When I wrote my eighth novel, as typical, I began to promote it months out from it even getting into the hands of my beta readers. I had named it *Picture Perfect*, and touted that working title all over social media. My readers began talking about *Picture Perfect* on their newsfeeds, asking me questions about it, and really helping to build up buzz for its eventual release. All sounds great, right?

Well, here is what happened – one of my beta readers told me she didn't like the title. I love my beta readers, and rely heavily on them for direction at the pre-editing stages. This feedback affected me in two ways.

Firstly, I cringed at the thought of having to change the title at this stage because I had marketed it so much already. I talked about *Picture Perfect* in interviews, blogs, on my website, and all over my newsfeeds. To rename this, and communicate this renaming, would take enormous effort.

Secondly, on a totally different tangent, I felt empowered that I could change the direction of this novel in such a dramatic way just by changing the title.

A working title is just that, a title that keeps us working. I can't say this enough – be flexible with it and be willing to change it. Also, be open to criticism on it. In fact, seek out critical feedback. Weigh it objectively. Play devil's advocate with it. Don't let your emotions rule your actions with something as critical as your work. You want to put your best out there, and to do that takes self-control to avoid the toxicity of self-preservation. Toss defenses to the side and listen to what people are saying. Is the feedback valid? If it is, let it sink in and do something valuable with this feedback.

The reason my beta reader didn't like the title *Picture Perfect* was because it was prosaic and left no room for imagination. The title, in essence, told a story in and of itself that left no mystery. A story should have turmoil, conflict, and hold the reader captive with its lure of what might be or what might not be. The title didn't match the story anymore. The story was not picture perfect. The characters faced tons of conflict that far dismissed any such nonsense of being ideal and perfect. The title simply didn't live up to the story. It didn't match the book. It didn't grab her attention.

She painted a picture for me:

"If I were in a bookstore looking for a new book to read, and I had never heard of you or read anything by you, I would skip over your book. I wouldn't even pull it off the shelf, because the title doesn't say anything to me. It sounds idealistic and hopelessly romantic. It sounds like it is going to be a fluff story, not the soul-searching journey that is your story."

After receiving this feedback, my gut told me this: My first step in marketing is to grab readers' attention, and if my title does not hook the reader, I'm not going to accomplish that.

Jump into Creative Mode

I needed to rename my book. My first reaction – *ugh*. I was done writing the book. Now was the time to pour myself a glass of sangria and kick up my feet. I wanted to celebrate the end of my fun journey frolicking through the brambles of literary landscapes, not recreate one of the most vital parts of the novel.

After I moaned and groaned for a few minutes, I got serious. I set aside my sangria, planted my feet back on the ground, and jumped into creative mode.

I would not come up for air until the *perfect* title struck.

I decided to make a list of concepts and emotions – words, phrases, fragments – that my title should convey. My lead character was on a journey to find herself, to find her value, and to understand her place in the world. She needed to understand how she related to her lover, her former lover, her friends, her career, and most importantly her inherent desires. So some of the ideas I listed included:

Journey | Dreams | Starting somewhere | Taking the first step
Removing comfort | Banishing routine | Opting out of stability
Taking that risk | Fork in the road | Start and the journey begins
Life doesn't happen until you let go

I stared at this list for several minutes, letting each concept filter off the page and take up flight in my subconscious mind. The theme of a journey to somewhere formed, and connected to my book's overall theme. As if the curtains of my mind opened and allowed the bright sunshine to cast its rays onto sleepy synapses in my brain, the title popped into my mind – *The Journey Somewhere.* It not only carried a bit of mystery, it also invited the reader to determine for herself what that journey started out as and what it evolved into.

Let the Brainstorming Begin

When brainstorming a book title, aim to play to potential readers' emotions and to spark their curiosity.

A great title must at the very least reflect the story's content, create intrigue, and elicit an emotional response.

Short and snappy titles have proven to be successful. Not only do they fit on the spine of a book without effort, but they also tend to be memorable.

Whether you're creating your book title prior to planning out your novel or after you've already written it, here is a technique that will spark fresh ideas.

This is what you'll need: A magazine and a computer.

For ten minutes, select a keyword or phrase from as many headlines in the magazine as you can and type them out in a column.

Make a second column. For ten additional minutes, repeat this exercise selecting different keywords or phrases.

Now comes the fun part.

Make a third column, and rearrange keywords and phrases from each column to make a unique title.

This is how I came up with my title for my third novel, *Tangerine Twist*.

After I planned out the story, I needed a working title. I wanted something that would represent the name of a special guitar my lead character's grandfather had given to her at a pivotal time in her life. When I saw tangerine and twist written together it clicked. I thought, what a cool name for a guitar!

Here comes a little extra notation on this title. Later on, I went to wash my hands and realized the bottle of hand soap on my sink was named Tangerine Twist. Fate? I like to think a little bit of fate was at play (smiles).

STEP 2: DEVELOP YOUR CHARACTERS

For a character to be memorable and stay in readers' minds long after reading your novel, a character needs depth and dimension.

A memorable character has:

A "tag"

A tag is a tool used to identify a character and set her apart from others in a novel. A tag can include physical traits, mannerisms, facial expressions, speech habits, or even scents.

A worthy purpose

Make it a purpose that is not trivial, but instead is filled with passion, ambition and values. What does she want out of life? And why does she want to achieve this goal?

A method

How does she deal with obstacles and conflicts? Is she a flight or fight person?

A viewpoint

How does she view the world? How does she interpret the behavior of others? How does she see the outcomes of her actions? As progress or failure?

A reason for her view

What happened in her life to shape her view?

A flaw

Every character needs to be flawed in some way, otherwise there is no growth. And readers want to see growth.

A redeeming quality

Even our villains need something that makes the reader want to keep reading about her actions.

Clashing motivations

Make sure she has goals and motivation that clash with the other characters. This increases tension and conflict.

Many writers like to keep a catalog of their characters. I do, too. I find it helpful to refer back to the catalog at times when the story takes over. It's at these times when I forget her eye color or that she loves rock music. It's the little details that bring a character to life. It's what bonds us to them and makes them pop off the page and become our best friends, our fantasy lovers, and enemies. It's what makes us yell at them when they are crossing lines they shouldn't be crossing and what brings tears to our eyes when they hurt or cause hurt to someone. It's what makes us want to slam the door in their face for acting so foolishly or hug them and never let go when they've acted selflessly.

Sample Catalog:

Demographics:
- Name
- Date of birth
- Height/weight
- Cultural background
- Hair color
- Skin color
- Eye color
- Physical traits

Personality:
- Sense of style
- Habits
- Hobbies
- Career
- Family relationships
- Friendships
- Enemies
- Childhood memories
- Greatest strength
- Greatest weakness
- Outlook on life
- One thing she'd never forgive someone for doing
- Person/being/thing she'd die for

- How character will change

- Ambition in life

- Story goal

- Conflict standing in her way of achieving story goal

- Epiphany that is catalyst to her eventual growth

A great way to get to know your characters before you start writing the book is to journal. Sit in a quiet place and start a journal entry from their perspective. Imagine you (your character) just returned back from a hard day at work. How does she feel? What did she wish would've gone better? How is she perceiving the smell of her apartment and the sights of it? Is someone there bothering her? Is she petting her dog as she writes? Is she crying? Is she smiling? Is she happy? Is she depressed? Get into her head. Let her take over the driver's seat. Allow her to unload her feelings onto that journal entry. Don't censor her thoughts. Let her run wild with them. Journaling is her safety zone. The one place she is free and safe to explore her true feelings – the ones no one else knows.

STEP 3: PLAN THE PLOT

Plot is what keeps the readers asking what happens next? It is the structure behind your novel that includes the pace and flow of essential ideas, introductions to characters, and deliberate revelations and surprises.

For a story to form, it must move from its current place to a new place, reached only by climbing over, trudging through, and bending around obstacles that keep the story moving and reshaping as the pages turn.

Browse the shelves of any book retailer and you will find dozens of different approaches to writing a book. Some people can sit down and type out their novel starting from chapter one, and continue on that tangent all the way until they reach the end. Others enjoy writing scenes out of order. Still others like to write scenes that may never even make it into the novel because, in writing them, their primary goal is to simply get into the head of their characters and find out where they should start off the story.

In writing a novel, my characters often take me on wild rides that I didn't plan. Nowhere in my strategic planning did I even think up some of the things my characters do. They take over, and sometimes, yet not always, I stick with their storyline over the one I labored with for weeks on end.

Flexibility is Key

Ideas often pop into existence in the strangest of ways. You might be sitting on a bus and look up one day to read a quote that clicks a switch in your creative brain telling you that you created your character all wrong. In these sudden moments, you taste the bitter dread that your plot line may be going in the wrong direction.

Many writers face this dread, and typically do right about the time when they've reached the middle of the novel. They discover that what they planned out originally creates a flatline effect to the story. To unravel from this situation requires flexibility and a willingness to change.

A Story Line Should Never be Forced

What might've looked great on a storyboard, doesn't always work once you get the writing muse pointing you in entirely different directions and opening up your mind to ideas that decided to wait until you dove into the story before they appeared.

That, my friends, is why writing is an art. There is no cookie-cutter approach to writing. If one existed, can you imagine the boredom that would riddle every reader?

That being said, even though a cookie-cutter approach to storytelling doesn't exist in any real sense, guidelines do, and these guidelines can help open you up to creativity.

The intuitive writer may enjoy a more *let's see where this is headed* approach to storytelling. She may begin her writing journey without a road map and let her characters discover the story for themselves. Many have been successful with this approach, and if it works for you, you must listen to your gut and do what is says. However, if you are more of a roadmap kind of person, then plan your plot.

When to Plan Your Plot

If you are more inclined to stick to a project if it's structured, then plan your plot. I happen to be one of those writers who needs some sort of direction and structure before I start writing. I like a plan, but I keep that plan extremely flexible. I've never written a novel and completely stuck to my original plot-planning. The characters always introduce me to new obstacles and situations mid-story. When they do, I honor these new ideas and allow them to inject their magic into the story.

But, true to my nature, I like structure. So, I get as much of my story ideas down, giving my wild, wandering mind a place to settle along the way of my novel's birth.

I like to think of my plan as a pearl necklace that can be changed around, realigned, taken apart and put back together again. The reason I enjoy the flexible structure isn't to limit my creativity, but to enhance it, shape it, deepen it, and to create a starting point, a middle ground, and a goal to reach.

I'm not one to jump in a car and just drive to see where life takes me. No. I like to map out my route. If I decide to stop and shop at a store from a sign I see on the roadway, then that's okay. I'm flexible. But I know I'm heading in the general direction still. My point B is out there, and after I'm done shopping, I'll get back on the road and head in that general direction. Without knowing I have a point B, I could ride in circles all day and get nowhere fast!

Here's another reason I plan. I need to know in advance that I have a storyline worth reading, even at the initial stage. If it can stand up at the initial stage, it'll certainly stand up once I start layering details and subplots into it. I want to make sure I have a set of obstacles that'll keep blocking my characters so that a reader will stay glued to the story to find out how the heck these characters get around these obstacles.

To engage a reader, a story needs to have more than a character going from point A to point B. The writer must create a compelling enough reason for this character to be traveling on a path that should be anything but easy and straight. It should be winding, sloping, uphill, and unpredictable. This path should have obstacles blocking the character from continuing onward.

In other words, this path, or major conflict, should give your character a reason strong enough to push her past that point of turning around and giving up.

The setup to this conflict should be introduced in the first scene of the novel. The reader should be asking a question by the close of that first scene, a question that will intrigue her until she finds out the answer. That question should poke her and prod her to turn those pages until there are no more pages to turn.

The story goal of getting past obstacles to get to that point B must be worthy and the actions believable.

Place obstacles in her path that keep her from achieving this goal throughout her journey. Force her to make some tough decisions and dreadful mistakes. Create compelling epiphanies and lessons as she bumps and trips her way through, in the pursuit of something greater than the limitations of her inner conflicts.

Create a problem that seems daunting and impossible to overcome; one that only this character can solve. She'll have to give up her firm grip on her current state. She'll have to grow, evolve, and find new balance. And for this to happen, she'll have to sacrifice a part of her old self to emerge as that one person who can solve the story's big problem.

Keep It Simple

A beautiful story need not be complicated and convoluted, dragged down by endless subplots, twists and turns. Some of the most vivid stories are those with simple concepts. A man loves his children and will stop at nothing to protect them from the harsh world. A reclusive woman finds love online and fears losing it if she reveals her true self in person. A singer makes it big and gets swallowed up in fame, losing the very thing she wanted all along, to be someone worthy of such accolades. Connect to a reader's emotions, and you've got your hook.

Add Depth and Realism

So how can you come up with ideas on how to add in these obstacles and worthy-enough conflicts to give your story that depth and realism it needs to become a page turner?

Devising a strong plot is probably one of the toughest and most critical pieces to crafting a novel. A lot of writers spend most of their time brainstorming their *pearl necklace*. Getting sucked into the vortex of writer's hell, where ideas are sucked out with little mercy and supposed little hope for recovery, happens easily. This is the place most writers give up – the point right before the first line of their novel is written. They become the frozen tendrils of an abysmal existence where logic forms too strong of a grip on imagination, choking the life right out of it. To rise above the frozen tundra of wordlessness, a writer needs a benevolent flow of ideas that can be brought on by artful planning.

Cultivate Your Creativity

Some writers are gifted with the ease of storytelling, while most others struggle to define their critical literary components. No need to stress at this early obstacle. Commit to staying the course, and you'll get there.

The point at which a writer decides to write a book, she typically would have some formation of a story taking up root in the garden of her creative soul. Just as with any garden, the land needs to be cultivated, pushed around a bit, tilled and toiled with until some of the stubborn weeds come to surface and are replaced with nutrients that will take that tired old soil to rejuvenating levels. Our creative minds are no different. We've got lots of clutter in there that needs to be sorted through and reenergized.

An Exercise to Cut Through the Clutter

Decide the theme of your story

Is your story about forgiveness, coming of age, romance, love triangle, death, coming to terms, friendship?

Decide on the lesson

What will the readers big takeaway be from your story? Will they learn to love deeper, take greater risks, let go, or advocate for something outside of themselves? What is the big lesson?

Decide on obstacles

Obstacles will force the character to move forward on her journey. They are necessary to give life to a character and offer the reader a reason to keep turning the pages. Obstacles should appear throughout the story and keep the character from achieving her goals. When deciding on what kind of obstacles to sprinkle into the story, be sure they are rooted in realism and cause the character to grow. Ask yourself, what drives the character to be in the place she is? What is preventing the character from just solving the problem head on? Why should the reader be worried for this character? What lesson does the character need to learn to be in a position to solve this problem?

STEP 4: CHART SCENES

When I first delved into writing a book, I experienced a severe case of middle-of-the-book lag. As a novelist, there is no greater tragedy than reaching that thirty-thousand word count and saying *I'm so $%^&*%*# bored*!

If you are that talented novelist who can start out writing chapter one and continue on a productive, engaging journey all the way up until the point when you write the end, then I envy you! Many intuitive writers have been highly effective at writing each scene in order, allowing the story to unfold as they type it.

If you're not like this, don't despair. There is a cure!

The Cure for Middle-of-the-Book Lag

Some writers may argue that writing a novel is a purely creative process. Creative, yes, it is. It's also mechanical, which is great news for those who fear they lack creativity.

The crux of a great page-turner is the ability to entertain your readers with a story that touches their emotions, gets their hearts beating, and piques their curiosity to the point that they have to keep reading so they can find out what is going to happen next. This kind of literary magic happens when a writer can take the reader on a journey that is filled with proper pacing. The key to proper pacing is planning it out and deciding where to place heart-stopping conflict, highly-emotional scenes, and light-hearted reprieves.

A novel that never allows for a break, can leave a reader exhausted. The same is true of a novel that never gets the heart racing. It can leave a person bitterly disappointed and bored, causing her to skim in search of something that gets her revved or causing her to slam the book shut and toss it against the wall in bitter disgust.

Create the Magical Balance

If you're systematic, then you'll probably love this next exercise.

The following information will teach you how to create a clear view of the big picture of the settings, plot lines, subplots, characters and pivotal scenes.

Chart eight to ten of your most exciting plot points before you write a word of your novel. Decide two things: The dominant action and the dominant conflict.

I like to use index cards for this part of the process. I plant myself in a quiet corner of a café or bookstore, and lay out my ten most pivotal moments. For a moment to be pivotal it must do at least one of these:

Create a problem for the character
Change the direction of the story

All of these pivotal scenes must logically point towards the climactic scene (the most intense and riveting scene in your novel), and ultimately to a resolution that leaves readers with a sense of awe and wonder.

I'll use my analogy of a pearl necklace for this exercise.

Decide what scenes will be most influential and plot them out, then tie in shorter transitional scenes as though stringing a pearl necklace. Just as when planning the plot, keep this string of scenes flexible. You may need to adjust as you go along, as the characters begin to take on a life all of their own. Their journey might be better than what you had originally planned. The basic structure is there: a set-up scene, seven to ten pivotal scenes that change the direction of the story, a climactic scene, and an ending scene.

I am a visual person, so I literally plot these scenes out on index cards and later plot them on a poster board where I can see them rise and fall in relation to each other. The scenes will vary in intensity where some are minor complications and others are major, off-the-chart complications.

I'll share my nine complication scenes from a brainstorming session I had when planning *The Muse*. The story inevitably took on a life of its own, and the structure changed slightly from these early charted scenes. However, in charting these scenes, the story stayed intact and on point with the overall message and theme of the book, which was to never stand silent when you have a voice.

What started out as a romance story, turned into something even more dramatic. The story evolved from these initial master scenes into a story that took on issues far extending beyond my original plans, issues like suicide, bullying, social psychology, and facing deep-scarring fears. Had I not spent some time plotting out the overall scheme, I don't believe my lead character, Jane, would've had the confidence to spread her wings and show me those important scenes that strung along beside these master ones – scenes that told her story in a way I hadn't planned.

The Muse
Master Scenes

Opening Scene | Happens in 10,000 words

One day, as her east coast corporate headquarters hosted their monthly meeting for all branches, in walks the new beautiful events manager, Eva Handel. Eva is everything Jane is not but wishes she could be – attractive and fun, and not a reclusive, shy, inhibited person who is afraid to blink in the presence of women. Eva shakes her hand and an electric shock runs through her. Jane can't look up at her. She simply blushes, bows her head submissively and watches as Eva skirts through the marketing department, shaking hands and leaving mouths agape in her wake.

Complication Set Up

Unable to stop thinking of her for days, Jane searches for her on Twitter and follows her. She takes in Eva's tweets, waiting for one with which she can play along. From behind a computer screen, she is free to be who she wants to be – an extroverted free-thinker, not afraid to speak her mind, instead of the overly shy, awkward girl she really is. When Eva sends a provocative tweet out to the masses, Jane jumps in and challenges her on it. Eva immediately follows her and the two start bantering back and forth.

Complication – No Turning Back | Happens in 20,000 words

Jane enjoys toying with Eva, and Eva keeps coming back for more. Then, Eva starts asking her personal questions about her life. Jane starts to embellish, creating a larger-than-life façade of the woman she really wishes she was. She claims to be a successful writer, then squirms to rework old articles she wrote in case Eva asks her for one. She claims to be athletic, then starts a home video program to get into shape when she reads how Eva admires health and fitness.

Complication – Surprising Twist

The flirts become more intense and Jane is sucked into them, unable to resist, surprising herself at how clever she can be and how her words are capturing the heart of someone like Eva. She's never been romantically involved with anyone, and has never felt the rush of euphoria from flirting. She's always been too afraid of women to have experienced this kind of attention from one before. The flirting affects Jane in a weird troubling way that sends her heart fluttering. Eva says gentle things to Jane that make her feel all sorts of love for her.

Complication – Tension Mounts | Happens in 15,000 words

Jane starts to get brave and send photos of herself. Of course, she takes them at provocative angles, hiding parts of her face and body, revealing only pieces of herself, the pieces she starts to like. Eva tells her she's beautiful and seductive, and this sends Jane flying high. No one has ever told her such a thing. This feeling is one she never wants to lose, and will protect with everything she can. So, as Eva comes to town for monthly meetings, Jane hides, fearful of being discovered and then destroying this great new joy and power source.

Complication – Tension Reaches the Summit

When Eva starts to ask her to skype and to meet, Jane freaks out. She's brave behind the computer, but would never live up to Eva's standards, surely. She'd never be pretty enough, never be articulate enough, and never be confident enough in person. The thought of standing in front of her and trying to carry on a conversation is deeply troubling. Her fear of being twenty-nine and never having been with anyone would be a big part of her insecurity. She's afraid to destroy this great image she's managed to create because she's afraid to bring back the real Jane, the geeky Jane, the one girls, pretty and outgoing like Eva, spat on, pelted with rocks, and teased. She doesn't want to reopen that pain. But she finds it impossible to resist Eva. The push-pull of this is painful and wonderful all at once.

Complication – Worst Nightmare | Happens in 25,000 words

As Eva presses on to meet her, Jane is overcome with fears and insecurities of rejection. She decides it's safer to withdraw and play up a busy lifestyle than to deal with the inevitable rejection. As a result, Eva pulls away considerably to the point she doesn't send private messages anymore, just public tweets in response to Jane's. Jane has never felt so hollow and empty. She'll adjust, she keeps telling herself.

Complication – Nightmare on Steroids

Then, tables shift when Eva starts to flirt with another girl in public tweets, an ex of Eva's. Jane is brought to the brink of her worst fear. She must choose: Fight for Eva by revealing herself and rising to the challenge of her fears or slip back and allow this great ride to end by hiding behind her insecurities for the rest of her life?

Climactic Scene

She shows up at a public event and reveals her true self, putting aside her own feelings for those of Eva and many others affected by her silence.

The Ending | Happens in 2,000 words

They go on a real date.

What Comes After Pivotal Scenes?

Once you've got the major points plotted, it's time to fill in the gaps. What happens in between the heart-stopping master scenes? These gaps offer the perfect places to add narrative voice, dialogue, tie-ins, and rest breaks, allowing the writer to control the story pace and the reader to catch her breath. But make no mistake, even though these scenes are minor in comparison to complication scenes, each one of them still needs to serve a purpose and hold a level of tension that will keep the pages turning.

Some writers prefer not to plan this far in advance of writing. Some would rather flesh out the complication scenes, and then have the freedom to write the secondary, connecting scenes without plotting and planning. Still others prefer to have an idea of where they're going, and may find success in loosely plotting connected scenes onto this storyboard.

Why Go Through the Trouble?

The whole point of planning your scenes is to avoid that boring, lagging middle of the story as much as possible. Stringing these scenes along an imaginary pearl necklace allows a writer to add the critical element of variety throughout the book, ensuring there are enough complications to keep the hum alive and to help avoid a reader ever muttering the words *who cares?*

This structure, even loosely based, will help maintain flow and help ensure all the pieces are pointing towards the answer to that ever-present story question that the writer planted in the reader's mind in the first scene of her page turner.

STEP 5: REFRAIN FROM EDITING

In the early stages of writing, specifically the first draft of a novel, many writers find it helpful to proceed without grammatical rules.

As novelists, we often get stuck in that editing phase as we write. This is common. It's also unproductive. Writing and editing take far different parts of our mind to perform. Writing requires creativity and flow to get into a productive zone. Many believe that a novelist does her best work when she writes freely without regard to grammar, spelling, and word choice. To get your tone and style out there in their most natural state, you have to allow for fluidity and freedom to take your creative brain on a journey past these rigid rules.

Rigid rules stop creativity in its tracks. It places limits on our imagination. It tells us to stop, analyze, and change before our words even have a chance to lift into poetic existence.

This is why the exercise of freewriting is so effective for many suffering from writer's block. When engaged in freewriting, we permit ourselves to ignore rules and let our minds take us on a journey where everything and anything is possible and where our natural voice comes out, allowing the magic to unfold.

Once you've gotten that first rough draft of free words sitting in front of you, then it's time to put on your editor cap and turn to the analytical part of your brain – the one that combs through the rubble and the clutter to uncover the gems we write as creative freewriters.

I personally write my entire first draft of a novel in freewriting mode. I let those red underlined words sit on my page. I let the run-ons keep running. I allow the awkward transitions to plop on the page and rest while I get my story down.

Once my first draft is written, then it's time to go through my scenes one by one and rip them apart, editing the heck out of them.

Writing and editing are two different processes. They should each get equal attention; just not simultaneously.

STEP 6: WRITE A SYNOPSIS

Whether you are submitting your manuscript to an agent, traditional publisher, or self-publishing it, a synopsis is an important tool to selling your book. Even if you go the self-publishing route, writing a compelling synopsis is critical. This will serve you in book interviews, in writing jacket copy, in writing sales information on your author page, and in offering that all-important tight nugget statement readers often ask of their favorite authors prior to a book release.

To many aspiring novelists, writing a synopsis can be harder than writing the actual novel! The reason is because it's concise and stripped of the details we are so used to providing in our written work. I have written a synopsis for each one of my novels. Yes, even though I am the publisher of my work, I still go through this critical step.

Here's why I go through the trouble: the synopsis is the first formal piece in my planning stages. I use it as a roadmap. It allows me to build in all the necessary story elements that an effective novel should contain: strong plot; overarching story question; subplots; major conflict; ambitions, goals, and desires of lead characters; obstacles faced; theme; and a strong, logical resolution.

Whoa, you might be thinking. *That's an awful lot of stuff to throw into a one or two page document!* To that I answer respectfully, if you don't know where you're going, how will you ever get there?

A synopsis is your roadmap.

Where to Begin?

Because the synopsis serves as a roadmap, I prefer taking full advantage of its purpose and writing it in the planning stages, after I've charted my scenes. Below is my process, chunked down into three steps.

Write a Nugget Statement

This is your hook. This is your one sentence summary that will test your discipline as you set out to write your novel. It is that one sentence you will send out to readers when they ask you the all-important question, *so what is your book about*? When someone asks you such a question, I estimate you have about five seconds to hook them. That's a small window.

So, with this in mind, it's best to keep your nugget statement to no longer than forty words. The purpose of it is to tell your story idea in as concise a way as possible. Imagine you are telling your best friend your novel idea and trying to explain, in as little time as possible, the main idea and conflict of your story and why she'd want to read it.

Here's an example of mine from my novel, *Inner Secrets*:

New roommates, Hope and Lucy, are crazy about each other, but neither is free to engage.

This one sentence tells a lot in no more than sixteen words. From this, we can extrapolate the main question readers will be asking as they read this book, which is: Will Hope and Lucy eventually be free to engage? It might also be conjoined with the question of: What will these two have to endure to get to this freedom stage?

This nugget statement is the driving force of your novel. It is the main thread-line that will weave in and out of your story's themes, conflicts, subplots, and character actions and reactions. Every sentence in your book will naturally point in its same direction.

From here, grow this statement to a summary paragraph, then eventually an entire page or two.

Write a Summary Paragraph

Turn the nugget statement into a summary paragraph. Include in this paragraph the elements of a beginning, middle, and end. I like to construct this paragraph in five sentences including, an introduction; the first, second, and third major conflicts; and finally how it all comes to pass.

Nugget statement:

New roommates, Hope and Lucy, are crazy about each other, but neither is free to engage.

Paragraph summary:

Hope Steele just destroyed her marriage, her integrity, and her freedom to pursue the life she was meant to live by cheating on her husband, Ryan, with a woman. Plagued by guilt brought on by her cheating, she seeks a fresh start by renting a room in an estate home with five other people from varying backgrounds. Hope is committed to being a better person than she was with Ryan, but soon finds herself deeply attracted to one of her roommates, Lucy, who is engaged to Adam, another roommate. What ensues is a dance between right and wrong. In the end, and for the first time in her life, Hope will understand the breadth of and secret to love and intimacy when she finally learns that the road to such freedom starts with being true and forgiving herself.

Write a Five Paragraph Summary

Write a paragraph for each sentence in your paragraph summary. So, in the end, you've got yourself five full paragraphs to make up your full synopsis.

Five paragraph synopsis:

Hope Steele is a thirty-year-old woman from Baltimore who just admitted to her husband of three years that she cheated on him and that she's gay. Understanding at first, Ryan tells Hope that her happiness is all that matters to him and that she can have everything, the house, the furniture, even their cat. He returns two weeks later bitter and requests they sell everything and go their separate ways. A woman she admires, Lucy, from work has invited her to move in with her and her fiancé and three other roommates. Afraid to cross that line again, she refuses the offer. She turns to her best friend, PJ, and asks if she can move in with her and her fiancée, Rachel. She does, but, they are trying to conceive and don't have the extra space, so they offer her a room for a few months. Now, instead of feeling empowered by coming out to Ryan and charting a new course, she feels displaced and horrible about destroying her character, her life, and her self-respect.

Plagued by guilt and self-doubt, she seeks a fresh start by renting that room in Lucy's estate home. Rooming with others is just what she needs because her nights have become bitterly unbearable. Maybe she'll even make new friends and carve out a whole new life for herself with them. When move-in day arrives, she is thrilled with her living arrangements. Everyone seems nice and harmless. Then, she sees Lucy, and a river of euphoria rushes in and tosses her around like a ragdoll.

Hope is committed to being a better person than she was with Ryan, but soon finds herself deeply attracted to Lucy, who is supposedly straight, even though she slips her a furtive, even flirty, smile when Adam isn't around. The two bond right away. They enjoy the same music, the same books, the same workouts, the same everything. Lucy opens up to Hope about many of the things she is lacking and insecure about, and Hope returns in the sharing. Then, in a moment of passion, Hope kisses Lucy. Lucy responds by telling Hope she's not gay and that's she's crossed a line.

To get her mind off Lucy and the horrible mistake she's made, Hope goes out on a series of dates. She winds up dating Nadeen. She introduces Nadeen to everyone, and Lucy just responds by showering Adam with more affection. This burns a hole in Hope's heart. She finds Nadeen to be dull and immature and can think of nothing but Lucy. But, she continues dating her because Lucy seems to be opening up again, seemingly comfortable by the protective barrier of Nadeen's presence. The attraction builds up again, and Hope can't help but to flirt back when Lucy flirts with her. Then, one night Lucy asks Hope to be the one she experiments with to see if she should really be with Adam. Not wanting to stoop to that low level again and be the one who Lucy will always regret someday, should she choose Adam, and not wanting to hurt Adam either, Hope refuses. This decision helps her to grow into a person in complete control now, a person worthy of respect and love, a person who values a commitment over a temptation. She understands that the pain of reversing back into the person she despised when she cheated on Ryan would tarnish any future that could come out of the moment of pleasure.

In the end, these two women learn to standup for what they believe is right for their hearts, and they come to understand the breadth of and secret to love and intimacy.

Things to keep in mind:
- Write the synopsis using the same tone and style of your novel. If your novel is funny, make your synopsis funny.
- Write the synopsis in the present tense, third person.
- Introduce your antagonist, protagonist, and supporting characters, describing what makes them tick.
- Describe your main plot line by telling the most pivotal scenes of your novel. A pivotal scene is any that changes the direction, increases the tension, and forces a character to act.

CHAPTER INSIGHTS

- Create a working title
- Be flexible and willing to change
- Seek feedback
- Create a catalog for characters
- Brainstorm emotions/concepts and string them together until one strikes
- Avoid ill-crafted pacing by plotting master scenes
- Build complication scenes that change the direction of a novel and/or create a problem for the character
- Ensure all complication scenes logically point to the climactic scene and ultimately a satisfying ending
- Visualize plot points like a pearl necklace, where each scene strings together to form a completed story
- Freewrite first draft to get to the meat of your story
- Refrain from editing as you write first draft
- Write synopsis and use it as a roadmap

Chapter Three

Develop Your Style

STEP 1: HOOK READER FROM PAGE 1

After asking many people what stops them from reading a book, the overwhelming answer is that the first page failed to grab their attention.

As writers, we have one page to dazzle potential readers and lure them to turn that page to discover what other surprises we have in store for them. Arousing a reader's curiosity requires an intriguing flow between characterization, beats, pace, and surprise. Characterization is the art of revealing the personality of a character. A beat is a literary tool used to add pause. It can slow a scene down to add dramatic tension and buildup. An example of a beat is adding action to a scene of dialogue to show the reader the effect of one character's words on another. Pace is a tool to control a novel's speed and rhythm. Surprise is that essential element that grabs a reader's attention and leaves her in a state of unexpected awe. Impregnate the reader with a fascination, and you've got her hooked.

As writers, we can nurture the lonely parcel of land in a literary landscape and turn it into something magical with the simple flick of a suggestive adjective or audacious parallel. We can sprinkle that field with as many wild flowers as our imaginations desire, not squelched by the demands of rules and worries that litter the so-called perfectly laid out lands before us.

The ability to create such literary cravings for readers is attainable, and quite readily I'll add, with the practice of a few techniques.

Wow from Page One

Create an Intriguing Statement

Nothing grabs a curious mind quite like an oddball phrase that catches one off-guard. Such clever engineering of words will drop jaws, cause instant onslaughts of expletive adjectives, and stop the world from stealing a moment more of the reader's time because she is too cued in to your fictitious world now. She will not be able to drop that book in lieu of sleep, housework, homework, television shows, or other important tasks because gosh darn it, you've created one heck of a burning question in her mind that has her reading onward to find out what the heck you meant by that first oddball statement.

Here's an example from Anne Tyler's *Back When We Were Grownups*: "Once upon a time, there was a woman who discovered she had turned into the wrong person."

I want to know more. Why did this woman turn into the wrong person? What wrong person did she turn into? What made her so wrong? And will she ever feel right again?

Plagued by these questions, I need to continue reading to find out. Curiosity is stoked after only reading one sentence. A mere seventeen words.

Create a shocking scenario

Readers love when we jolt them. They want to be taken off balance. They want to shudder in pleasure or horror. They want to utter statements like *seriously* and *I didn't see that coming.*

A clear example of how this is accomplished can be found in *The Death of Bees* by Lisa O'Donnell: "Today is Christmas Eve. Today is my birthday. Today I am fifteen. Today I buried my parents in the backyard. Neither of them were beloved."

The offspring of such a sentence is undoubtedly sheer mystery. Is this child suffering? Will she be loved and nurtured? Why did she not love her parents? Did she kill them?

Create an alluring character

Characters are people our readers will bond with throughout the sentences, paragraphs, and chapters of our stories. They will be people they want to know more intimately. They will become their best friends, their secret crushes, and their muses. Our characters should jump off the page and become three dimensional in our readers lives. Create characters who readers will crave to spend more time with by adding a layer of undeniable magnetism.

Take this interesting character introduction in Dodie Smith's *I Capture the Castle*: "I write this sitting in the kitchen sink."

I don't know anyone in my real life who would be sitting in her kitchen sink writing a letter. I'm instantly pulled into this whimsical character's world, scratching my head at her daily motives to thrive in a world so obviously mundane to her own.

After reading that first sentence, I wouldn't be able to put the book down without getting to know this person a little better. Move over to-do list, I've got a mystery here to solve; a mystery that dictates I put aside my judgments and fears, and allow this spectacle before me to unravel herself and bring me into her world for a little while.

Confess a secret or an intimate thought

Intimacy builds relationships. It is the fabric that weaves a friendship or love together, binding us in an intangible force that repels all that isn't sacred or affirming. Sharing intimate thoughts ripens us to feel on a level that far outweighs the threats of potential distractions. When we share, we invest in each other and in the magic that encircles the invisible energy. We crave to connect, even in literary form. We crave to learn more and be the keeper of secrets for those we adore, respect, and love. Create that kind of intensity between your readers and your characters, and those pages will figuratively turn themselves.

Ray Bradbury does a brilliant job with this short, to-the-point first sentence in his novel *Fahrenheit 451:* "It was a pleasure to burn."

I feel instant sympathy for this character, wanting to nurture his broken soul and learn what carved such a dark thought in his mind.

Tap into the senses with intense sensory description

Supply a reader with the right amount of sensory detail and she'll experience your world as if she lived and breathed in it along with your characters. Invite her in by teasing her senses, and you'll whet her appetite for more. Let her smell the aromas, feel the heat, hear the echoes, see the artistic palettes, and taste the succulence.

Here's an example of how this is done well in *The Namesake* a novel by Jhumpa Lahiri: "On a sticky August evening two weeks before her due date, Ashima Ganguli stands in the kitchen of a Central Square apartment, combining Rice Krispies and Planters peanuts and chopped red onion in a bowl."

I can hear the crunch, taste the fruition of this crazy concoction, and sense her craving for something deeply seeded within. Now my mind fills with theories of which I need to test. And, the only way to test those is to indulge further into this story.

Write a provocative or sexual moment to stir strong emotion

Sensuality calls upon our deepest emotions, toying with them until we release ourselves into literary submission. We love to feel the soft beating of our hearts as we engage in intellectual dances with words on a page. Our minds reel over sexy innuendos. Our bodies want to tango with the emotions stirring on the pages of a gripping, provocative scene.

John Updike's clever first sentence in *A&P* illustrates how, even with just a few words, a writer can brilliantly set the tone for the story: "In walks these girls in nothing but bathing suits."

I'm intrigued. Need I say more?

Start with an unusual situation

Most of us love to be tickled with mystery. We love to guess what lies beyond the curve in the road, and won't stop moving forward until we discover it for ourselves. Perhaps it's the little child in us that keeps us poking under and around obstacles to discover if we were correct in our guesses.

Here's an example from *Snow Child* by Eowyn Ivey: "Wife, let us go into the yard behind and make a little snow girl; and perhaps she will come alive, and be a little daughter to us."

I'd love to stand in that snowy yard, secured behind a tree, and peek in on these two characters who actually believe they will make a child out of snow.

STEP 2: CREATE CONFLICT

As a reader, one of the most disappointing things to run into would be a story with no point. I've read a few, and when I have, I've yelled at the pages asking why on Earth nothing was happening. I want to see someone struggling, dammit! I want to sweat out a scary situation, cry over a disappointment, and flex my fists along with the characters as they push through obstacles to find their true paths.

Readers crave conflict. We want to see our favorite characters fall down and rise up to face their fates. We want to see them win the tough battles, whether that battle be on the eleventh floor of an office building facing the office protagonist head-on in the personal battle of her life, or in the midst of a shaky relationship where one tough choice leads to a new set of tough choices that ultimately carve her into a deeper, more enriched person over time.

Writers have a tough job because we not only have to create believable, relatable conflict where our readers can feel every sense our characters are feeling, but we must do this without being contrived and causing our readers' eyes to roll in disbelief and frustration over outlandish attempts to force silly conflict just for the sake of fulfilling a novel's top need.

What Is Conflict?

A difficult, even seemingly impossible, choice for your main character

Does one run toward an obstacle to save a life or away from it to save another one? What if you had to decide between embracing your dream and walking away from it to protect someone else's dream? What if the only way you could save your friend's life was by risking your own?

These are the tough questions that get pages turning. Readers want to know what is going to happen next. They become deeply entrenched in the lives of these fictitious characters, feeling every ounce of their frustration, sorrow, and ultimate joys. As writers, we are artists of the barren landscape that once occupied our computer screens. Fill that screen with tough choices, nail-biting scenarios, and fist-pumping situations, and you've got yourself a page turner and the opportunity to grow an incredible readership.

An obstacle your character must overcome in order to grow

To navigate a winding road takes skill, tact, ingenuity, tough skin, and emotional intelligence. When one takes such a trip, she changes. She has no choice. The person she started out as at point A will always be a different person when she lands at point B. Readers want to see this evolution in a character. They want to meet someone to whom they can relate, learn from, and become intimately close with as they turn the pages and the character reveals their true self – the person they are without the makeup and social disguises.

Readers want to grow to love this person you create. For that to happen, this character must be dynamic; be willing to fall down from grace; and be strong, fierce, or stubborn enough to get back up again to show the world what she's made of. Readers want to cry tears of joy when they realize the character before them is just like them – real and flawed. When they get to the end, they want to be able to smile, and perhaps nod on the recognition that is displayed before them, the recognition that we are all human beings with issues and the ability to evolve and grow from these very issues.

A character's fatal flaw

We've all seen ourselves, our friends, and our loved ones make mistakes over and over again out of a strange loyalty to the status quo. Why? Because the status quo is comfortable. It is a place of recognition and a place to rest our feet, kick back, and close our eyes to the fears that lurk in places we don't want to look. But what happens when we allow these fears to hold us hostage in a life of safety? We sit idle and watch as the rest of the world passes us by in pursuit of ideals that are greater than fears.

Flaws bind us to a holding pattern. They are our bad habits that pin us down and fight us every step of the way. They dictate how we live life and how we interact with the world around us. A fatal flaw is a character's weakness. It is her stubborn grip on the world – a grip that holds her back and keeps her from reaching her goals.

Creates an imperfect character who readers can relate to and root for to overcome a challenge

No one wants to read a book with a character that is one-dimensional and perfect. When everything about her is smiley and pretty, we want to rip up those pages and scream out in frustration for money and time wasted on its investment. When she has no flaws, we groan and shake our heads. When everyone else around her carries the flaws instead of her, we cringe. That is just not how life works. Leave out conflict, and you kill the story and any possibility that a reader will make it to the last page without skimming, skipping, and leaving a bad review to ensure no one else suffers.

Everyone is flawed. Perfect people simply don't exist. When people pretend they are perfect, they repel friendships, love, and any semblance of a genuine relationship. Even if they appear to have it all, something deep inside lurks at the root of the soul.

People relate better to each other when they can air their vulnerabilities and share empathy. The same is true of flawed characters.

Make your characters real, honest, genuine, flawed people, and readers will relate. Make them believable by giving them a bad habit, a warped way of thinking, anything that says *hey, I'm real! I've got some flaws going on just like you do!*

Readers want to see the underdog rise to the occasion. They want to see characters overcome the downward spiral tendencies present in all human beings. They want to cheer on your characters and be there at the end to whisper, if only hypothetically, congratulations my new friend, you did it. You survived. You overcame. You won!

Build Conflict

Play the *so what* game

One of the first things I do when planning my novels is I start asking the question, *so what*? If my follow up to this question is *well, if XYZ happens, everything changes*, then I've landed on a productive path to creating conflict. If my response to *so what* is a simple shrug or *well, nothing*, then I keep plugging away until my mind creates a strong enough conflict to keep the story moving along.

Example from *The Fiche Room*: When planning *The Fiche Room*, I declared the main idea would be that Emma Hill falls in love with a beautiful woman named Haley. I had nothing more than that. I knew I wanted to write a romantic tale involving two beautiful women, but that was all I had. Obviously, not exactly a page turner. I asked myself, *so what? They fall in love. Big deal.* I then answered my own question with a follow-up one: *Well what if Emma is engaged to her high-school sweetheart, and is taken off-guard by her growing affinity toward Haley?* Bingo. Story evolves. Conflict ensues.

Toss in a problem

Ask yourself what your main character wants more than anything in the whole world. Then, determine three psychological reasons why she can't get it.

Example from *The Fiche Room*: Imagine if the only way you can be with the one you truly love is if you risk hurting two other people in the process?

Emma's blocked by (1) her guilt, (2) her inherent need to please others before herself, and (3) her deeply engrained fears of societal reactions to her decision. The tension these inner conflicts cause keep the story moving along and the readers connected and rooting for Emma to choose what's best for her and not for others. Throughout the novel, Emma feeds this inner conflict by acting in ways we'd expect someone to act if she were trying to cover up guilt and spare other's disappointment.

Move the story forward

In other words, the conflict can't be trivial. Leave the meaningless dribble out of the story, and instead fill it with purposeful arguments and challenges that cause the character to react in a manner that pushes her toward the eventual goal. She needs to change through an epiphany gained only by experiencing the conflict.

Keep characters on the edge

A comfortable character results in a boring story! Never let her get too comfy. Tease her with comfort, by all means, but be sure to pull that cottony soft blanket off her just as the bitter cold draft blows in. Let her taste the sweetness of victory, but be sure to feed her the bitter candy before she leaves that banquet. Toss tables around as she meanders through a crowded hall, so that her path resembles nothing straight and easy.

STEP 3: DAZZLE THE SENSES

Nothing is going to flatline a reader faster than a long, drawn-out passage about how the setting sun reflects its warmth on the leaves, which line the lake, which is filled with lily pads upon which… blah blah blah. I almost made you drift off there, didn't I?

Just as every character and every piece of dialogue should have a purpose for remaining in your book, so too should every detail when it comes to setting. It needs to serve a purpose more than just filling white space. It might be helpful to remind yourself that the goal of writing the setting is to place your reader smack dab in the center of this world you are creating. You want the reader to taste, smell, feel, hear and see the space your characters occupy.

To do this right takes a bit of balance. As you can see from my example above, you don't want to over describe and risk boring your reader. But on the other hand, you don't want to under describe and take for granted your reader can feel, taste, smell, hear, and see everything that your character is experiencing.

Balance Details

Indulge in sensory overload

To be convincing in your delivery, you have to experience the deep feelings of the setting you're trying to create. If you're writing a scene that takes place in a park, sit still for several minutes, close your eyes, and place yourself in that park. What does the grass feel like under your feet? Can you taste the sweetness of the spring morning? Doesn't that lilac bush smell just like your aunt's yard when you were younger? Do you hear the sound of that wonderful laughter? How would you describe that to a friend?

Get in touch with the sensory details of the setting you are describing. Some people have a hard time conjuring up details like this, especially if they've never experienced such sensory delicacy. In a case like this, you must rely on your imagination. You must draw upon sensory details with which you are familiar and create a convincing setting from that.

Just as an example, I've never stood on a stage and strummed a guitar, singing to thousands of eager fans. But, my character Becca sure has, and I needed to set the stage, so to speak, for her. How could I do this when I've never experienced a situation like that? Well, I dug deep into my memories and pulled out of them similar situations that brought me the kind of euphoria Becca felt each time she picked at her guitar strings and the crowd applauded her. For me, I recalled the first time I stood before a room of my college peers and delivered my first speech. Another one I fired back up in my mind was the time I graduated college, walked on the stage, and shook hands with the president of my university.

You see, even if you haven't specifically experienced a situation, you can pull from similar ones to capture the emotions you'll need to write compelling fiction.

Paint a clear picture

Sit still, close your eyes, and embrace the feelings that show through for you. Once you've got a mental image, you'll want to paint this same image for your readers by writing it out in a way that'll tap into their senses.

Here's an example of what I mean by painting a clear picture using the senses: You could say, *it was a spring morning*. Or you could make this really stand out by saying this instead, *the air smelled like a freshly sliced cucumber*. The latter sentence uses the sense of taste and smell.

This brings me to an important point. Don't be afraid to tap into many of the senses when painting a moment for your reader. Use more than just the sense of sight. Add in another one or two senses to layer the realism.

Leave out trivial details

Bringing us back to the point I made earlier about over explaining, toss out the details that don't matter. Such commonplace descriptions will just drag out your setting paragraphs and bore the reader. Leave out the obvious things like green leaves, black road, or brown mulch. Instead choose to go beyond the natural with the goal to create a sense of awe and belonging to that place. **An example**: The dog's yelp echoed through the lush, moist forest, competing only with the squawk of birds weaving in and out of the canopy of banana trees.

Paint a clear picture, and your reader will taste, smell, feel, hear, and see exactly what you intended.

Use metaphors and similes

A metaphor is one of the most visual, transformative tools at a writer's disposal. It allows the reader to see and imagine a detail with such acuity, the character actually transforms before us. But it must be used sparingly, as it will detract from the novel's story and credibility if overused. **An example of a metaphor is:** Sara was a delicate, lacy blanket, safeguarding the child from the perils of his abusive bullies.

We know Sara isn't actually a delicate, lacy blanket, but we know how one would make us feel in the face of discomfort and angst. That image will stay with a reader for pages on end, each time Sara is mentioned. We'll grasp without a doubt who Sara is as a person, and how her energy swaddles us in everything warm and inviting.

A simile is a slighter play on imagery than a metaphor. The couch was like quicksand, pulling me in and embracing every part of my tired body with its relentless grip. In this example, we're comparing two sides of a subject – the couch in its inanimate state and the image of quicksand and its movement around the object.

STEP 4: TAKE A STANCE – POV

The voice(s) that tells your story must be strong enough and ring true for a reader to latch on and remain tightly focused for the entire novel. The voice of the novel is what the readers will bond to, learn from, and engage with on levels that touch some of the farthest reaches of their imaginations. Which point of view you choose is based on your own style of writing. The one constant though, you need to select one and stick with it!

First person

One character tells the story. The reader can only know what's going on inside the character's mind. The entire worldview is from this point of view's perspective. It is one of the most intimate storytelling narrative voices because the reader is brought into the emotions of this storyteller. We are right there in her mind, along for the ride, feeling every high and low, every bit of regret and torment, every tear shed and giggle released.

What I find personally fulfilling about writing in the first person is how intimate and personal I can be with the character when revealing her personality.

Some writers find this limiting and difficult to do because they can only speak of the action that is happening in front of the character. First person uses the pronouns I, we, and us as a narrator. A story told in this point of view can be told in present or past tense.

Third person

This point of view involves a narrator's view of the world that the characters live in. It is how we naturally perceive the world and tell stories about what's happening to others with whom we interact. I like to imagine the person telling the story in third person as someone's shadow, always standing right there next to the characters, seeing and feeling everything they are experiencing, and telling that tale to others as she experiences it.

Just as with first person, we are catching a glimpse into the intimate life of our character, however the difference here is that the writer and character are not one in the same, but rather the constant companion seeing and perceiving the events unfolding before her.

The greatest benefit to this point of view is that, every once in a while, this shadow can leap around from one character to another, shadowing many to get glimpses that she can then share in a story.

Third person narrative is much more flexible in terms of storytelling. This point of view uses pronouns like he, she, they, them, and it. A story told in this point of view can be told in present or past tense.

Omniscient

Another realm of the third person point of view is the third person omniscient point of view. Third person omniscient is a method of storytelling in which the narrator knows the thoughts and feelings of all of the characters in the story, as opposed to third person limited, which adheres closely to one character's perspective.

Through third person omniscient, a writer may bring to life an entire world of characters. Think of the voice being outside of the story, and knowing everything about the characters and the events in their lives.

Another way of understanding this storyteller is as one who is all-knowing, rather than limited to the character she is shadowing at the moment. Through this voice, a storyteller can choose to reveal as little or as much information to the reader as desired. For this very reason, the omniscient narrative is risky because you may kill the dramatic tension that keeps the story alive.

STEP 5: CREATE EFFECTIVE, BELIEVABLE DIALOGUE

The truth of the matter is this, dialogue can make or break your novel. If it's awkward, stiff, and uncharacteristic of your characters, you risk losing your reader.

If it's done effectively, your characters will come to life on the pages and your readers will connect to them, root for them, cry with them, laugh with them, and want to continue being a part of their fictitious lives.

Writing effective, believable dialogue can be achieved with some simple techniques.

Show don't tell

To help readers experience the world you have created, you must take them by the hand and lead them. You can do this by introducing them to the mysterious forces, the inspirational settings, the charismatic characters, the crazed actions, and the uphill battles that weave into your storyline. Show them and make them become as much a part of the landscape as your characters are. Position your words in such a way that the reader can actually imagine being a part of those pages and not just an observer reading the letters.

To show and not tell means a writer must use action in her voice and avoid passively tossing adjectives, adverbs, and verbs around that clog the motion and don't give us any real sense of true emotions.

Always aim to add a human aspect to your words rather than just stating facts. Don't just tell the reader someone is pretty. Describe in detail using language that evokes strong emotions around the state of prettiness how this character is in fact pretty. Instead of just stating the obvious, *she is pretty,* draw in a reader by saying something more along the lines of, *her caramel colored hair, wavy and wild, flirted with her golden skin.*

Here's another example: Rather than stating in a passive voice, *she was angry*, try inviting the reader in by saying, *she marched towards the front of the classroom. "I'll show you exactly what I mean."* As a reader, we sense the anger seeping in as she marches her feet up to the front of that classroom.

Dialogue is a great way to show emotion. But remember, emotion comes more often from the action tags used around dialogue. What I mean by tags are *action* markers. *"I don't care about what your mother thinks of my job," he said, slamming the door with his foot.* This is a great technique to "show" the reader how the character is feeling without just stating the emotion. Should all dialogue be presented with action tags? Absolutely not! Too many tags can slow down a scene. The best way to test dialogue flow is to read the scene out loud.

Dialogue offers a great way for a writer to describe her lead character. When describing characters, try having other characters describe them for you. *"I love your hair like this." Emily plucked up one of my wispy highlighted pieces and twirled it between her fingers. "Keep it long and full of waves as it is now. It's incredibly sexy."*

Now the reader has a clear visual of the POV's look, AND because it's also *shown* with action and sensory detail, the reader can feel and see clearly how this character looks.

Use nonverbal patterns to communicate

A fun way of showing your character is agitated is by tapping into nonverbal communication. *She clenched her jaw and narrowed her eyes. "I'd be happy to do that for you."* Without having to tell the reader this character is in fact not at all happy, we show her instead, and we can feel her icy stare and closeted feelings.

Stay true to emotions

Dialogue offers us a great way to capture emotions. The timing of dialogue can speed up, slow down, and add clever chaos to a scene. Increase urgency by staying true to the character's emotional state. If she's upset, choose short, snappy sentences that are void of fluff. Keep the reader speeding along with her thoughts by using forceful verbs and sentence fragments.

To slow down the reader, perhaps in a scene where she is enjoying a sentimental moment, use longer, more relaxed, unhurried exchanges. Or create action around the dialogue that is more leisurely, lingering and thoughtful.

Use action

Use action to avoid using too many dialogue tags when indicating a change in speaker. Dialogue tags are *he said* or *she said*. Shake it up in the dialogue exchange by adding in some action tags too like, *he moved to her side. "I know what you mean."* We get the sense that he is comforting her.

Avoid small talk

Every piece of dialogue must have a purpose. None of it can be dull or unnecessary. It should never be fluff, unless fluff is purposeful to show off a character's personality, motive, or reaction to something. If it doesn't move the story along, get rid of it.

To avoid small talk and keep the flow between characters in dialogue, always set out to write it with a clear goal for its purpose. Are you building sexual chemistry, embarking on a fight, creating a bond, or digging for info? Every spoken word needs to point to that goal. Try to avoid using blank phrases like *how are you today? Oh, I'm good. How are you?* That does nothing for a story, for characterization, for setting a scene, or for building conflict.

Try this technique to writing dialogue

Some writers find a blank page intimidating, especially one they want to fill with snappy, purposeful conversation. If you find yourself staring blankly at nothingness, try to write a few poignant pieces of dialogue from a particular scene first, then build to and away from it. I often like to write a piece of intense dialogue from the middle of a scene, then my mind asks the question, *what happened right before this to make the character say that?*

Also, try getting into the POV character's head. Imagine you are having the conversation with someone. How would you feel? What sounds would you hear? What sights would you see? What emotions are you experiencing? Put yourself right there in the scene, and let it play in your mind first. But, be sure to have something to write with because that's when the ideas and brilliant dialogue will come at you! It never fails that these snippets of dialogue come to writers when they're out walking and have no opportunity to write anything! That's when having a recording device comes in handy.

Additionally, as you're building the scene, take some time to read it out loud. You'll be amazed at the emotions that will come over you, and you'll find better ways of saying things.

CHAPTER INSIGHTS

- Create a burning question in readers' minds
- Create three-dimensional characters
- Develop believable, relatable conflict throughout the story
- Make readers want to know what's going to happen next by including tough choices
- Develop dynamic, flawed characters who are willing to fall and get back up again
- Ask *so what* to check for valid conflict
- Use sensory details to place reader into the story
- Choose POV and stick with it
- Show, don't tell, to lure readers into your story
- Give purpose to every piece of dialogue

Chapter Four

The Art of Fine Tuning

STEP 1: SELF-EDIT

So, let's say at this point that you have a first draft written of your novel. Perhaps you've printed it out and are thinking to yourself, *wow, I wrote a book!*

Completing this phase of a book project is a great feeling. Embrace it. It's one of those few moments as a writer that causes pride to swell, and if you've pushed through to complete that first draft, then you deserve a moment to cradle that beloved novel to your chest and cherish it.

Many people say they are going to write a novel and never do. Well, you did it.

So now what? What comes next in the process?

Chances are high that, just like every single writer on the planet, the manuscript you are holding in your hands is full of grammatical errors, typos, and inconsistencies. That's completely normal and expected.

Hire an editor now, right?

Yes. But not so fast.

Before a single beta reader or editor peruses your hard work, comb through it with fresh eyes. An editor will find these issues, sure, but remember that an editor's time is extremely valuable, and you'll want her to put effort to its greatest use. Clogging an editor down with too many errors, errors that can easily be fixed by you, is a waste of her time and your money. An editor's job is to uncover those problematic areas in the novel that, as a writer, you can't see easily. You'll want her fresh eyes to find the real issues in your manuscript versus bogging her down with silly errors that swallow up her time and energy.

Furthermore, if you send such an error-riddled manuscript to beta readers, you'll lose out on the gem-filled advice that they are able to provide. Beta readers are phenomenal at offering first-hand, targeted readership views on your story. You want them focusing on the story at hand, not the errors. The feedback you want is on context, plot, characterization, flow, and logic of your story. So, you'll want to polish up your manuscript as best as you can before sending to beta readers.

Self-editing checklist

I have a checklist of words that I run through my 'find' feature in Microsoft Word to help me self-edit. I simply plug these in and comb through each one to improve or correct them.

Give action to adverbs that end in -ly

Adverbs have their place within the context of a novel, but they should be used with caution. They often drown out verbs, causing passages to flatline. Rewrite them by turning them into action verbs.

Example: *He walked confidently.* These three words are grammatically correct. They make sense. But, could they be stronger? Absolutely. *He charged forward, eyes focused at the podium on the stage.* The reader can feel the charge and imagine the confidence of this man.

Delete unnecessary exclamation points

This punctuation element tells the reader the character is excited about something – tells is the operative word. A few exclamation points sprinkled throughout a novel is absolutely fine, and can add strength to a passage. Overuse it, and it dulls. Try rewriting the sentence with an action verb instead.

Example: *I peeked through my eyes. "Wow, the umbrella is red!"* As a reader, I feel I should be excited that the umbrella is red, yet I have no idea why. I don't feel a strong reason to get excited about it. *I peeked through my eyes at the umbrella. "Wow, you got the red one." I twirled around and hugged her, squeezing her and squealing, blown away by her personalized gift.* Now the reader is transported to that room and the intimate moment. She can hear and feel the mounting excitement, and learns even more about the relationship of these two characters just by an added sentence. No exclamation point needed to drive home the emotion.

Rewrite drowning verbs

Do a search for the following drowning verbs and turn them into action-oriented ones: think, seem, believe, feel, give, hold, make, and was. I've provided some samples from my novel, *Staying True*. The examples presented represent my first draft. The rewrite shows how I tightened up the original sentences and saved them from drowning, rejuvenating them with more punch and expression.

Example: *I braced my hands on the counter, **thinking** that I should just run and never look back.*

Rewrite: *I braced my hands on the counter and fought the urge to just run and never look back.*

Example: *Her carefree spirit **seemed** natural and rooted in something more pure than a dance club with techno music and strobe lights.*

Rewrite: *Her carefree spirit reached up out of the darkness like fresh sprigs blossoming in early spring, rooting itself in something more pure than a mere dance club with techno music and strobe lights.*

Example: *I truly **believed** it was because she was unavailable that we continued to pine for each other like rabid wolves.*

Rewrite: *I surmised we continued to pine for each other like rabid wolves because that's what two selfish, cheating people did when given the chance.*

Example: *I kissed her under the apple tree, **feeling** more free and alive and one with nature than I ever had.*

Rewrite: *I kissed her under the apple tree, blossoming to a new awareness that tickled my core.*

Example: *Her hand softened in mine, warming my core, **giving** me an enormous feeling of love and gratitude.*

Rewrite: *Her hand softened in mine, warming my core with her love and affection.*

Example: *This woman would **hold** me on a pedestal, equal, if not higher, in height to that of the one my father **held** my mother.*

Rewrite: *This woman raised me up on a pedestal equal, if not higher, in height to that on the one my father placed my mother.*

Example: *We blanketed each other in soft kisses before we climbed out of bed, hand-in-hand and **made** our way to the kitchen for coffee and overfilled bowls of Honey Nut Cheerios.*

Rewrite: *We blanketed each other in soft kisses before we climbed out of bed hand-in-hand and strolled into the kitchen for coffee and overfilled bowls of Honey Nut Cheerios.*

Example: *Her hair **was** all wild, blowing around her face.*

Rewrite: *Her hair blew around her face in wild persistence.*

Do a Homonym Search

Run a search for the following words to ensure you've written them correctly:

- your/you're
- our/are
- lose/loose
- breath/breathe
- to/too
- who's/whose
- then/than
- their/there/they're
- chose/choose

STEP 2: WHY WRITERS NEED EDITORS

An editor is a coach. She keeps you in check. She sits you down and has honest dialogues at times, telling you where you've gone wrong and what you must do to get back on track. She cautions you at times for using the wrong tense, point of view, and spelling of common words. She may laugh with you when you've done something silly like overused a word to the point of nausea or plugged in a completely wrong name for a well-developed character.

She is there to gently remind you that you are supposed to enjoy this process of writing and not view it as a torture chamber, which it sometimes feels like when words evade our creative minds. She is there as that whisper in your ear, urging you to say no to dinner and drinks with friends and say yes to get your writing goal accomplished for the day.

She is there to mark up your manuscript with her fancy red pen, cautioning you with pain-staking detail about how you need to tighten a scene, remove a sentence, add a comma, remove a comma-splice, and destroy the repetitive cathartic scenes you have written to drive home a point no reader in the world wants to read.

She helps prevent the threat of readers rolling their eyes in angst over contrived moments where your characters dig themselves into a situation and miraculously run into a saving grace.

She wants to protect you from evil reviews. She wants you to succeed. She wants you to call her up or email when that five star review pops up on Amazon and jump around her living room floor with you as you squeal in delight that someone mentioned the brilliance of a character's action, an action your editor proposed you polish up and present in a great light.

Your editor is your saving grace.

She is the secret behind your brilliance.

Don't get me wrong, your editor may at times make you cry, make you angry, and make you want to scream out frustrations through a mega phone so everyone in earshot can hear just how challenging she is and how unfair you think her advice is at the time. This is natural. This is necessary. This is writing!

You want your manuscript to come back to you highlighted in red words and covered in comments. That is the sign of a great editor. You don't want to hire an editor who pats your back and massages your ego. That's the role of your readers! If you are serious about writing, and want to grow to be the best one you can be, then you must open your mind and take the ego blows a great editor offers.

The editing phase is your chance to turn a good idea into a great one. Editors come in all different styles. Some are harsh, some are sweet, some are gentle, and some are extremely firm. You need to decide what type would work best for you. I personally prefer someone who is empathetic and respectful, but firm in her delivery. I crave knowledge, and demand timely, correct, and constructive criticism.

Most important note here is that you must trust your editor. You want to hire someone who is more knowledgeable than you at grammar. You want someone not afraid to criticize you. You want someone who has pride in the finished product. You want to know that at the end of the day, your editor reviewed your work with eagle eyes and a desire to help you improve your work.

Why Can't We Just Edit the Book Ourselves?

A curious thing happens when we spend months to years working on a written piece. We become intimately involved with it. And just like with any intimate relationship, we tend to overlook things and see past flaws.

Every good writer experiences this.

That being said, if you want your story to shine, you need to rely on the objectivity of someone detached from it.

What If You Can't Afford a Professional Editor?

For many aspiring writers, hiring an editor may not be in the budget. However, whether your goal is to self-publish your book or pitch it to a traditional publisher, you will need that second pair of eyes. Don't skimp on this. Budget this into your project.

Bottom line, if you want to be taken seriously as a writer, and you expect readers to pay for your work, then you need a professional editor. If a book is littered with errors, you may likely lose credibility and thus, your readers. A writer needs readers if she wants to be profitable.

If you absolutely don't have the cash on hand to hire an editor, there is a solution if you're able to find someone willing to travel this path with you.

Find someone you trust who can be objective and challenge you. Preferably, someone well-read, someone not afraid to hurt your feelings, or someone willing to perhaps go probono until a profit is made. Draw up a contract that states you will pay this person a fixed percentage on any profit made until an agreed upon editing fee is met.

So say you have agreed to pay the editor a $500 editing fee for her service. Perhaps you can make an agreed upon contract that states you will pay her a fixed percentage of profits until that $500 is paid in full. At the end of every tax year, send her a year-end summary of percentages paid and amount still owed to her.

I don't know any credible editors who would work for free. So, at least this way, you and your editor can grow the book together and have a vested interest in its success.

Writing and the Editing Process

A lot of writers ask what my line of operations is when it comes to writing a book. In a nutshell, here it is:

- I perform any necessary research. For instance, with the book I am currently brainstorming, preliminarily titled *The Dance*, I am reading well-researched books written by leading experts in the honeybee world and am also meeting with a local beekeeper and experiencing the honeybees firsthand. I want to get a firm grasp on everything and anything to do with honeybees. I want to intimately connect with them, understanding my eventual lead character's fascination and devotion to them.

- I write my first draft in free-writing mode, not stopping to edit. This process typically takes me four months.

- I step away for one to two weeks.

- I revise into a second draft. This process typically takes a month.

- I repeat revising until I'm confident my story is readable. This takes roughly another month.

- I have a team of beta readers read it and provide their gut reaction on things like: flow, pacing, believability, tension, overall plotline and character development. This process is roughly a month long.

- I take this feedback and let the suggestions marinate to a point I can effectively analyze them objectively without any defensiveness. I stay true to my story, while remaining open to ways to make it shine even brighter. THAT IS CRITICAL. This can take me anywhere from a few days to a week or more.
- Now I revise again. This typically takes a week or two.
- I send to my editor. She uses track changes to polish the manuscript by correcting grammar and punctuation, as well as reworking any awkward sentences. This is usually a month process.
- Once I receive edits back, I review the track changes and accept or reject them. Depending on the amount and extent of changes, this can take a few weeks.
- The last phase of this process is proofreading. Some editors provide this service as part of their package deal. Some don't. If your editor doesn't, you should either hire a proofreader or, if it's not in the budget or at this stage, ask a trusted reader friend to proof it for any leftover errors.
- Once you receive proofreading back, make any changes.
- Print out the manuscript and read aloud. THIS IS CRITICAL. I do this because I can hear mistakes more accurately than I can see them. In this phase, I'm correcting any lingering final grammatical or punctuation oversights.

I can't urge you enough to not skimp on this critical writing process. You want to get your book in its best possible shape, using the help of fresh eyes and perspectives from objective people, before you release it to the masses. Once it's out there, it's really hard to backpedal on negative reviews. People can be cruel. You don't want to fuel that cruelty with the ammunition of mistakes that could've been easily fixed before the public's eyes landed on them.

I personally have learned this the hard way. My earlier books had editing issues. I didn't always use this process. I released books with just my eyes and a friend's reviewing them. This resulted in errors. Thankfully, as a publisher, I was able to have these earlier books re-edited and re-released. It's a costly mistake that I hope I can help you avoid.

STEP 3: FIND AN EDITOR

What should you look for in an editor?
- Someone with whom you are comfortable
- Someone with whom communication is collaborative, respectful, and honest
- Someone who will respect your author voice and not change your story to match her tone and style
- Someone who is able to critique your book with tact so she is not destroying your confidence as a writer

Where can you find such a professional?

- Search elance.com or guru.com for editing professionals
- Ask for personal recommendations from writers in your circle of influence
- Visit the message boards on Writer's Digest, the World Literary Café, or other popular writing sites
- Search the members section of professional writing organizations
- Meet editors at writing conferences

Before you hire an editor be sure to:

- Take a look at her portfolio. How are the books she's worked on doing in the marketplace? Are the reviews critical of the book's editing? Look for red flags in this critical due-diligence step. Be sure to sample the book's first chapter to analyze the work for yourself. Do you see mistakes? Does it flow?
- Request a sample edit of one or two pages to evaluate the editor's editing style to see if comments and edits are productive. After she's reviewed your sample, ask what level of editing she feels your book needs. Does it just need light editing, maybe rewriting some sentences and proofing errors or more substantial heavy editing to tighten the story, fix subplots, advise on pacing and transition issues, and correct major grammatical errors? If you strongly disagree, seek another opinion.

- Negotiate the price and the timeframe upfront. Prices vary widely, and editors charge differently: some charge by the word; some charge by the page; some charge by the hour.

ONE-ON-ONE – ADVICE FROM THE EXPERTS

I sat down with editors JoAnn Collins and Ashley Martin from TwinTweaksEditing.com to ask them a few critical questions on the editing process.

Q. What does a good editor do?

JoAnn & Ashley: A good editor asks what the author's needs and goals are, and is able to make suggestions or point out potential issues, all while keeping in mind that the final call ultimately belongs to the author. This person becomes your partner. There is a relationship that builds between an author and editor over time. An editor will learn your writing style, getting into the head of each character, deeply envisioning the scenes and surroundings, and will suggest changes that enhance the story rather than take from it.

Q. Why do I need a book editor?

JoAnn & Ashley: Your story is a part of you and a reflection of you. You have created it, molded it, built the characters and scenes. You know it inside and out, and because of your close relationship with it, it's difficult to be objective. An editor doesn't know your intentions for the characters, how the relationships are supposed to play out, or the words you wanted to choose. In a way, your editor is reading your book the way your future audience will, but with so much attention to detail that she is able to help you identify issues with subjects like continuity and grammar, or anything that might not be completely cohesive. A second set of eyes will ensure that you are polished for your audience, helping to create a strong following and good reviews.

Q. What can I expect from a book edit?

JoAnn & Ashley: A large part of what you can expect from a book edit comes from what you *want* from your editor. Maybe you prefer to use the serial comma. Perhaps the point of view changes throughout your story. Or maybe you want to specify your editor's level of involvement by setting parameters or encouraging them to edit freely. Don't be afraid to communicate your preferences – this will save time and potentially get you to publication faster.

Expectation can also depend on which editing level you choose. Reviewing the specifics of each service will help you to know what kinds of changes could come back to you. Regardless of your preferences or service level, you will at the very least see suggested edits, comments and questions. You might also expect correspondence between the time of submission and the due date if questions arise that could affect the rest of the story.

Q. What is the most important consideration in selecting a book editor?

JoAnn & Ashley: Opinions differ when it comes to what is most important when choosing an editor. Some look for speed, while others focus on reputation or cost. These traits are valuable, but above all, choose an editor you can trust. Consult with other authors for referrals. Or if you have an editor in mind, ask if anyone else has used his or her services. What was the experience? It could be a friend or a stranger who lives on the other side of the country, as long as it's someone you trust to provide objective feedback and communicate with you as needed.

Q. My manuscript has already been professionally edited, but there still seems to be a problem. Should I invest in a second edit?
JoAnn & Ashley: If you feel there is still work that needs to be done with your story, it is entirely up to you to decide the benefit of a second (or third, or fourth) edit. If you still have time before publication, maybe you'd like to use an additional editor for a fresh set of eyes or new perspective. If you've gone through one round with your editor, and have made extensive alterations, a second round with the same editor could also be beneficial to capitalize on her familiarity with it.

Has your story already been published? What are the reviewers saying? If they're mentioning issues like typos, poor grammar, problems with continuity or such, the option is always there for you to submit your book for one more edit, likely improving what readers have to say.

Q. Are book editors usually qualified across the board or do they specialize in specific areas?
JoAnn & Ashley: All editors should be generally qualified. You are paying for their service, so don't be afraid to ask for their work history,

degree, and any other qualifications *you* feel are important. If you're writing in a specific genre, you may want to search for an editor who specializes or already has experience in it.

Q. What types of editing are available?

JoAnn & Ashley: Although editors might use slightly different terms, there are generally four types of editing: developmental, copyedit, proofread and polish.

Developmental editing is exactly what it suggests. The editor helps you flesh out characters' features, traits, habits, desires and flaws, and suggests ways to strengthen scenes and surroundings based on the senses. Is the bar's music too loud for conversation, causing the characters to have to share personal space in order to be heard? Can they smell each other's cologne or laundry detergent? Maybe one happens to notice a freckle that can only been seen in close proximity. Perhaps the other wrinkles her nose and pushes up her glasses when she's nervous. You can take the development of your story so far, but it's a good idea to have a different perspective to ask the questions you might not think of.

Copyediting focuses on the high level of language and style improvement. At copyedit, you might expect to see questions regarding word choice in order to avoid unnecessary repetition or to improve rhythm. With this stage, sentence structure might be improved upon when the editor suggests reordering the words for a better flow. Often times, this level of editing will include elements checked at later stages, but with the main focus being on the higher level.

Proofreading is typically a level of editing that follows copyedit. The scope of what is sought out is therefore smaller, likely including issues such as spelling, grammar, punctuation, consistency and readability.

A polish is ideally the last check before a book is ready to be published, or potentially an edit that occurs after publishing if the author discovers there are still issues and wants to take the opportunity to make changes and re-upload. At this point, the editor looks for glaring mistakes like typos, blatant inconsistencies and formatting errors.

Q. How do I determine which type of edit I need?

JoAnn & Ashley: You could still be writing, or maybe you've finished. Now what? Some writers have beta readers to help them flesh out characters and scenes, enhancing when needed and trimming what does not add to the story. Other authors utilize developmental editing for this purpose.

If you've narrowed down who you want to use for an editor, feel free to have a discussion with her about what stage you're at and let her help determine which level of editing might be right for you. Since each editor might offer slightly different services, consulting with your editor in specific can help both of you make sure you're on the same page, resulting in the best working relationship.

If you are still in search of an editor, see if the editors you are interested in have websites. Quite typically, the services offered will be laid out on their website and can help you identify which level of edit you will want to ask for, should you decide on that editor. Also, this can provide you with more tools to start a conversation with the editor.

CHAPTER INSIGHTS

- Review entire manuscript using self-edit checklist
- Perform a homonym search
- Choose an editor as a critical member of your writing team
- Budget editing into your book's project
- Create a process that works for you
- Perform due-diligence research before hiring an editor to ensure you are deciding on the best person for your needs

Chapter Five

Before Introducing Your Book to the World

STEP 1: CONSIDER YOUR PUBLISHING OPTIONS

Your novel is in its finest shape now and ready for the world to read. What is your best option to get it in front of readers? Should you seek an agent, find a traditional publisher, self-publish, or publish solely as an e-book? Each choice has its pros and cons. One common thread is that regardless of which route you take, you will have to put on a marketing hat to spread the word.

Traditional publishing with the Big Five

Simon & Schuster, HarperCollins, Penguin Random House, Macmillan, and Hachette are the publishers who make up the famous Big Five.

To publish with one of these mega publishers, a writer will most likely need an agent, as they rarely accept unsolicited manuscripts.

Most of these books have a great chance of getting into major booksellers like Barnes & Noble and Books-A-Million. The author is likely to receive an advance, and the publisher takes on the costs of production, distribution, warehousing, editing, design, etc.

Also important to keep in mind is that a writer doesn't retain full control over her work. Additionally, a writer gives up a significant portion of her royalty to agents and the publisher. It can also take years for a book to be released once accepted.

Mid-sized presses

Mid-sized presses, although not as well-known as their Big Five counterparts, still have name recognition and clout. Many of them exist and are often focused on niche markets. Most mid-sized publishers, but not all - especially with niche markets, seek agented submissions.

Small-sized presses

These small, independent publishers often provide a great opportunity for new authors to be discovered in a niche market. They are often nurturing and work with a writer to gain as much success as possible.

Their size, though, makes it hard to compete with the larger presses, often resulting in less exposure, availability, and sales. Their distribution may be narrow, which impacts the ability to obtain professional reviews and bookstore presence. Authors are expected to carry most of the marketing burden themselves.

Self-publishing

Many writers have found great success with this path, provided they invest in creating quality content and presentation. The author's cost for this can be zero to thousands to pay for specific things that many aren't able to do themselves such as editing, layout, and cover design.

To be successful in this publishing capacity, a writer needs to be diligent, determined, and extremely disciplined, not to mention open to independent learning.

If you are going to go the self-publishing route, it's critical to hire a team of professionals to get your work into its best possible shape. A lot of writers are eager to get their work out there without going through the painstaking details necessary to put out a quality piece. The result of rushing the process and not hiring a competent team to help get your work in that pristine state is the possibility of bad reviews that will remain forever.

I can't urge writers enough to polish their books to the best of their ability before setting them free to the public.

Personally, I publish my own books under my LLC publishing company, Sunny Bee Books. I prefer having full control over my work, including copyright, design, editing, and financial rewards.

That being said, this comes with LOTS of work and a willingness to invest in professional resources. This includes subcontracting an editing team, beta readers, CPA, and web designer.

Additionally, a writer choosing this route must invest a lot of time in promoting and branding.

The win for this publishing option is that the writer grants herself full control over her work, as well as full share of her royalties.

The drawback: Most large bookstores such as Barnes & Noble and Books-A-Million only stock books that are returnable. Self-published books generally use print on demand companies to print their books, and these companies generally don't have a cost-effective method for returns.

Vanity publishing

I will never endorse this avenue as long as self-publishing is an option. Vanity publishers are costly. These companies make their money from the authors, not by selling books.

They set premium prices on their books. And unfortunately, readers will not pay a premium price for a book from an unknown author.

In my opinion, a writer is much better off going the self-publishing route and investing funds to take care of the things she can't do herself like editing, rather than pay a vanity publisher tons of money to set a book up for commercial failure.

E-Book publishing

This is a huge market that continues to grow thanks to devices like the Kindle and Nook.

E-Books currently have high profit margins because they are not tied down by production, distribution, and warehousing costs.

Just as with print books, a writer needs to invest in editing services, cover image, marketing jargon for the book blurb, and possibly even layout services if not familiar with this. A writer also needs to work hard at promoting e-books as the market is emerging with new writers by the minute it seems.

P.O.D. publishing service providers

Print-on-demand technology has opened the door for self-published writers. Instead of having to invest in running a huge print run and storing that print run in a warehouse, the book is only printed when it is ordered. The primary P.O.D. providers are CreateSpace, Lightning Source, and Lulu.com.

CreateSpace is owned by Amazon, and books printed through them are available on Amazon, one of the largest online book retailers in the world. They offer low production costs, short turnaround time, no setup fees, no minimum orders, no inventory or warehouse fees, and it's a free DIY system.

Lightning Source is owned by Ingram, the biggest book distributor in the U.S. This is the option to choose if you are seeking the possibility of selling your book in a local bookstore. They do not guarantee placement in bookstores, but the possibility exists.

Lulu.com sells books on their own site and posts them to Amazon, Barnes & Noble, and other online retailers worldwide. Overall, lulu.com receives good ratings from its users. The biggest complaint I've seen rests in their pricing. Being that the price per unit is high, the profit margin is greatly diminished for the writer.

My Personal Reflection on Publishing

A publisher can help take many burdens off you, provided they take that kind of care with their authors. Not all do!

My advice, if considering working with a small press, specifically, is to read their book samples provided on Amazon. If you see a trend of their work having editing issues, I'd look elsewhere. No book is perfect. But if there are editing issues, they should be addressed/corrected and mentioned in the comments of any bad reviews to show the publisher is aware and taking corrective action.

Do your research. Ask them for references of others they publish, and talk to those writers to get their feedback. This is your baby. You want the best home for her.

For in-depth resources into publishing options, I recommend checking out: www.sfwa.org/other-resources/for-authors/writer-beware/small/

STEP 2: HOW TO SELF-PUBLISH

If you choose to go the self-publishing route, there are a few essential tasks you will need to complete to be successful.

Fully-edited manuscript

Your book will need to be fully-edited and in its best possible shape. As a self-publisher, you will not have the luxury of an editing team behind you as you would with traditional publishing. Be sure your manuscript is in its finest shape before considering to publish it.

Although technically you have the option of going back over it once you release it, this is not a default you want to choose. Once it's released and read, you can't take back the negativity that may spring from a poorly edited book.

Book cover design

If you have the budget to hire a professional book designer, do it. The book cover is your most important real estate. It can literally make or break the ultimate success of your book.

If you absolutely can't afford to hire a professional book designer, study cover art of existing successful books and add elements that resonate with you to your own cover. I don't mean copy! I mean study, analyze, and use elements such as font, size, colors, placement of author name, and white space in your design. Use programs such as Word, Photoshop, Illustrator, InDesign, or Canva to design your cover. For print versions, you will need to save your book cover in the highest quality. Industry standard is 300 DPI, color mode CMYK. For e-book covers, you will need to save your cover art in color mode RGB and 72 DPI is typically fine.

I'd like to recommend DIYbookcovers.com if you want to design the cover yourself. They provide templates and guides to help.

Required manuscript format

You will need to format your manuscript various ways in order to upload to popular retail sites. I personally layout my manuscript for Kindle, CreateSpace, and Smashwords. Smashwords will adjust my file to fit the following formats: epub, mobi, pdf, rtf, irf, pdb, txt, and online reader. Smashwords offers the Premium Catalog listing which reaches major global retailers. Once your book is accepted into the Premium Catalog, Smashwords automatically distributes it to major online retailers such as Apple, Barnes & Noble (U.S. and U.K.), Scribd, Oyster, Kobo, OverDrive, Flipkart, and Baker & Taylor, among the most notable.

Blurb

The blurb is the sales description potential readers will see on retail sites when they browse your book. It is the content you will likely place on the back of your book cover. It is, in essence, your book's lifeline to success. Just like the book cover, the blurb is your chance to stand out from the crowd and appeal to the emotions of a reader. It is that magic statement that defines your book in the space of a paragraph, or two at most, and what will ultimately determine if a reader decides to peek further into the pages of your literary brilliance.

If you've done your homework and written a synopsis, your job at writing the blurb will be easier. Pull from the synopsis those critical elements that address the main themes, the story question, and the major conflict. Keep it concise. Keep it true to the voice of your story. And most importantly, keep it interesting. This is the hook of your story, and you want it to reach out and grab readers' attention.

An exercise I would recommend you perform is to analyze the books on Amazon that resonate with you. What about their description appeals to you? How does the writer give you just enough, yet not too much, to hook you into clicking that purchase button? Also analyze books that, in your opinion, have a weak description. Why is it weak? Whatever your answers, avoid them when you're writing yours! Sometimes analyzing the mistakes of others offers us a greater lesson than solely analyzing the good stuff.

Keywords

Think of keywords as a navigational beacon paving the pathway for readers to find your books in the thick of the competitive ocean that makes up this wonderful world of publishing. You've written a great book, designed a beautiful, captivating cover, formatted your manuscript properly, and provided a smashing blurb that will surely hook readers the moment their eyes scan your clever eloquence. Fantastic! But none of that matters much if you're looking for sales and haven't provided those magic keywords and categories that'll lead readers to you. The concept of *build it, and they will come* doesn't apply here. You need to build it, then you need to take readers by the hand and focus them in on your book much like that lighthouse beacon dancing on the edge of a rocky shoreline in dense fog. With well over a million books selling on Amazon alone, you need to help your potential readers find a way through the proverbial fog. A great way to do this is to tag and categorize your book properly.

According to Amazon's KDP, writers can increase a book's discoverability by adding accurate descriptions and keywords. Relevant keywords can boost a book's placement in search results on Amazon.com.

Amazon allows for up to seven keywords or short phrases, separated by commas. They recommend combining phrases in a logical order (i.e. health and wellness nonfiction instead of nonfiction wellness and health.)

A good way to gauge the validity of keywords is to do a search on Amazon using those keywords. What kind of books show up? Are they similar to yours? If not, consider new keywords.

Amazon provides examples of useful keyword types:

- Setting (Colonial America)
- Character types (single dad, veteran)
- Character roles (strong female lead)
- Plot themes (coming of age, forgiveness)
- Story tone (dystopian, feel-good)

Categories

Amazon allows for up to two book categories. Think of a category as a shelf in a library. On what two shelves should your book reside?

When deciding which category best fits your book, consider conducting some research. Go to Amazon and browse books in the category you think best fits your book. Then, scroll down to the book's detail page to the "Look for Similar Items by Category" section located at the bottom of the page. Do these books match your book in scope? If so, you're likely in the best category.

Amazon recommends selecting the most specific categories and not general ones. Customers looking for very specific topics (i.e. Fiction >

Lesbian) will more easily find your book, and your book will be displayed in more general categories as well (i.e. Fiction > General). Amazon's advice: only select a "General" category if your book is actually a general book about a broad topic.

Author Central

If you are selling your books on Amazon, which you should be, use this wonderful feature! By creating a profile on Author Central, readers can learn about you, access your full list of books, watch videos you create, gain access to your blogs, see photos of you, read about your tour events, watch your Twitter feed, and connect with you on your website. In addition, writers can see timely sales data for free, including sales trends over time and where in the U.S. and U.K. your books are selling.

Every author should have their profile on Amazon. It's free, easy to use, and a great marketing tool.

STEP 3: DEVELOP THICK SKIN

There are two types of rejections that writers face, and both are equally as painful. One is from a publisher or agent rejecting our manuscript and the other is from readers who have rejected our work in a review.

The time to prepare emotionally for the rejection process is before you submit your manuscript for consideration to an agent or publisher, or if self-publishing, before you hit the publish button.

The one piece of advice many writers hear is that you need to develop thick skin. This is a lot easier said than done, especially if you happen to be an overly-sensitive person like myself.

A rejection letter or bad review can be heart-wrenching. To me, both are like a sucker punch in the gut. I've been known to cry after reading a bad review, and sadly I've let them destroy my writing for a period of time, sometimes a day to an entire month. Some reviews can be so personal in attack that they make a writer question her validity as an artist. I've experienced many moments hunched over the question of whether or not I should be writing in the first place if someone I don't know can slam me with words the way an abuser slams a victim.

Well, that kind of self-pity has never served me well. I toyed with the idea of never allowing myself to read another review again. But, never reading reviews again would not serve me well either. I've learned a great deal from them – the good and the bad ones. I do believe critical reviews are a great tool for writers, as they teach us things. They've taught me to think more like a reader when creating character motives and personalities, when deciding on plausible causes and effects, and when providing a character satisfying closure. I've learned what resonates and what doesn't by reading reviews. Reviews are another teacher to me. I value them when they are honest and respectful.

Learn to Handle Rejection

Acknowledge your feelings

You are a human being and you hold your work close to your heart. So it's okay to feel the burn after a rejection. All the positive affirmations in the world will not erase the sudden jab to your heart after reading someone's negative or critical review of the work that you labored over for months to a year. You will feel the pain and sting. That is natural. That is part of learning and growing. Without pain, we are stagnant and apt to become complacent in our actions. Absorb the pain. Allow yourself a set amount of time to feel it, then let it go.

I've cried over rejection countless times. I can't read a negative review and instantly let it go. I am not wired in that way. I don't know too many of us who are. We are sensing, feeling beings. Accepting your feelings makes it easier to deal with them.

Realize you can't please everyone

This is very hard to swallow for those of us who are pleasers by nature. We want to spread our love of the written word to the masses and appeal to everyone. We want jaws to drop, tears to be shed, laughter to erupt, and lovely accolades to flow from readers. Society programs us to go out into the world and expect great things to happen. So when we put ourselves out there and read someone's harsh words about our work, it rattles our core and dismantles all the confidence we've so diligently worked to build in the moments leading up to hitting the publish button or the send button on an email to an agent or publisher.

We expect great things to happen after that action. And when it doesn't, it deflates the ego like a pin to a balloon.

The known fact is that this world is made up a variety of people with varying backgrounds, experiences, and filters that have been carved through years of living individual lives. Not one of us is alike, not even a set of twins. Not everyone in the world loves the color blue. Yet, those of us who love blue will not stop loving blue because our neighbor dislikes it. We all come packaged with different experiences that affect our emotions on different levels. Some people love horror books, some despise them. Does that make the horror genre despicable in itself? Ask the millions of horror book fans out there that question. You see, there is something for everyone. Not every reader is going to love your story. Accept that and your career as a writer will become that much easier.

Opinions are not facts

We are entitled to form an opinion. Be grateful for this freedom. The wonderful element of a literary opinion is that it can often spark interest in readers who may have otherwise overlooked your work. Call it an intellectual challenge, but when I see a negative review, I sometimes want to read the book just to see for myself! Opinions, especially if well-formulated and presented with conviction, can be an advantage to writers. Reading opinions is also a fantastic way to get into the psyche of a reader's mind. We get a first-hand glance into what readers like, dislike, find believable, find ridiculous, and on what they are or are not willing to invest their time.

Another thing to consider is that even the greatest writers of all time receive negative reviews. Their work is torn apart in public debates and classrooms across the world.

Learn from the negatives

It is a difficult thing to learn from critical judgment, but not impossible. With most, the sting is too deep within the first few days of reading a critical review to be able to draw any sensible objectivity from it. Wait a few days and reread the review. This will allow emotions the time to simmer. Taking away the emotions allows us to evaluate truths. If there is something of value in a critical review, you will likely find it when you are viewing it through relaxed, unaffected eyes. Once you're at the point of objectivity, try hard to unearth any buried value, and honestly ask yourself if you can do better with having unearthed this valuable insight. You will grow significantly if you can open yourself up to criticism.

Focus on the positives

Just as a writer can expect negative reviews, we can also expect wonderful ones too! I print out every single one of my favorable reviews and read them from time-to-time. Nothing builds up a bruised ego like reliving the high of wonderful praise. Just as we have things to work on as writers, we also have those elements of writing that come natural to us and should be celebrated. Reminding ourselves of what readers like most about our writing is just as important as understanding repetitive flaws.

Never give up

I've sunk to low levels after reading unfavorable reviews, but I've learned that people can only have that affect if allowed. Some reviews are going to be harsh and mean. They are going to cut you down, rob you of positive vibes, and stomp on your heart. That's the writer's life, and the risk we all take when we share our work with the public.

Thankfully, I've grown thicker skin from my earlier publishing days, and I've applied all the advice I've given throughout this section. This has helped me get through the attacks of reviewers who are more like bullies than critical intellects. The world is full of mean and cruel people. That is fact. It is a fact every writer needs to accept or else fall victim to their insults.

These people do not deserve that kind of power over you. The moment you realize this, you set yourself free to create art. The world needs art. So, I beg you to never give up on your writing dreams because of something someone said. If there is validity to their rejection, learn from it and apply it, but don't let it crush your spirit.

Never let rejection letters or bad reviews make you feel inadequate as a writer or that you should somehow give up on your dream. The only way your dream ends is if you let it.

Write a Mission Statement

I'm going to draw upon a personal experience that propelled me to take a good, hard look at why I write. I asked myself:

- What if no one reads this?

- Is all of this hard work and sacrifice worth it?

- Should I be spending my time doing something that will offer me a more secure flow of income?

- Am I being selfish taking time away from my loved ones to hibernate for hours on end, typing a story that may never spread across the pages of a book?

Most every writer has these questions at some point.

I certainly did. In fact, I almost quit writing altogether because I didn't know how to answer these questions.

Several years back, after writing my third novel, *Tangerine Twist*, and after having it and my other two novels, *The Fiche Room* and *Two Feet off the Ground*, rejected by countless publishers, I sat with two of my friends and announced I would quit writing.

I was done.

I worked for almost five years writing those three books, sacrificing time, money, and emotions for what?

Under a blanket of stars, I sat on their patio and told them about the rejection letter I had received that afternoon for *Tangerine Twist*. The publisher told me it didn't fit their needs – the impersonal sentence every writer dreads.

I sulked like someone just cut off my legs and told me I'd have to crawl around for the rest of my life.

My emotions flooded my brain that night. I couldn't see past the riptide. It pulled me under and tangled me up into one heck of an emotional mess. I couldn't see past the relentless waves or feel much other than the pounding of rocks against my naked soul.

I sat before my friends, half a glass of wine in hand, as a washed up writer. And, darn it, I hadn't even taken my first baby step into the land of rejection!

The writing life can be brutal. It can wreak havoc on our emotions, causing us to sit like dried up rotted logs on the side of a churning oceanfront if we let it.

If we let it. That's key.

I needed to get a grip, and fast.

Thankfully, I had a set of loyal friends who talked some sense into me. They stared at me with frank eyes and asked me:

- Do you write because you enjoy it?
- Do you feel excited when you write?
- Even if you inspired one person by your words, wouldn't that be enough of a reason to continue?

Wow. Talk about a series of loaded questions.

My answer to all of those questions was yes. YES. I have stories to tell. So many I wish I had fifty hours a day to write them.

Just because a bunch of publishers rejected my books didn't mean my life as a would-be-writer should die. Who were they to have such power over my future?

I had dug out a grave and tossed myself into it before I even weighed my options.

What happened in the moments following this new energy surge changed the course of my life. I'm going to quote one of my all-time favorite motivational speakers, Les Brown, to explain the prominent thought lifting me to my feet that night on their patio and raising up my half glass of wine. "It's not over until I say it's over."

Later that night, I went home and formed a mission statement, which, to this day, hangs on my office wall: *As long as I encourage, inspire and enrich at least one individual with each story I write, then I will stay committed to this unique and exciting path I'm fortunate enough to be on.*

This mission statement immediately put to rest any question of my purpose or reason for investing my time and energy in writing.

Less than four months later, and halfway into the first draft of my fourth novel *Inner Secrets*, I sat at a financial planning convention to learn how to invest my money. The speaker presented his investment strategies, and at the end of his presentation, revealed a slide with a book on it. He stood directly in front of me, and as if speaking directly to me said, "I encourage everyone in this room to write a book. It is the most cathartic experience."

This multi-millionaire investment professional went on to explain that countless publishers rejected his manuscript and would only be willing to publish his book if he changed several key factors of it. He, being true to his inner entrepreneur, carved his own path, and self-published it on Amazon.

Call me ignorant, but up until that moment in time, I didn't even realize self-publishing on Amazon was an option. I just marched along in life assuming I needed a publisher to give me a hand in jumpstarting my writing career. Right there, under the spotlight of a blaring overhead and the sharp eyes of this smart man, my excitement bubbled over. I saw a possibility, a light, a new path. I sped home, and despite having just sat through fourteen hours of financial education, I fired up my laptop and looked into publishing with Amazon. The very next day, I opened up my account with CreateSpace and KDP. Fast-forward several months later, and all three of my books, formerly rejected by all publishers in my genre, soared to Amazon's bestseller list, and thankfully, have found their way back to bestseller rankings over and over again ever since.

Remember this: If your mission is personal and rooted in something greater than money, readers will find you. Your authenticity will be felt in their hearts.

I urge you to write a mission statement. It'll be one of the most important things you do as a writer. It will help ensure that rejection never gets a chance to cloud your desire to make it as a writer.

CHAPTER INSIGHTS

- Do your due-diligence research on publishing options
- Determine which publishing option is right for you
- Browse Amazon's KDP guide for useful information on formatting and marketing your book
- Look into the Smashwords Style Guide for great tips on correctly formatting your book
- Hire a book designer if you don't have the skill set
- Prepare for rejection before submitting your work for review
- Never give up on your writing dream because of someone's opinion
- "It's not over until I say it's over." Les Brown

Chapter Six

Branding Yourself

You've published your book. The time to sit back and relax is not now. Now, it's time to pump up your energy so you can build a readership. The only way your book is going to get read is if readers can find you. This step in the publishing process is probably the most difficult and time consuming of all. Branding yourself requires focus, thought, and consistency.

Amazon is flooded with new books daily. A writer can lose herself quickly in this thick forest if she doesn't learn to stand out from the crowd. Great, solid writing alone will not lift a writer to unique levels where readers can easily spot her. In addition to writing a top-notch piece of fiction that will leave readers breathless, a writer also needs to carve a well-lit pathway so others can join her along her writing journey.

This can best be achieved in four ways: a quality website, social media relevance, content curation, and lead generation.

STEP 1: BUILD A QUALITY WEBSITE

A website is your home base. It is the place readers will have access to everything you have to offer, including links to your social media platforms, blogs, media listings, photographs, list of books and access to purchase them, biography, videos, contact form, and ability to get on your mailing list for future announcements.

Your website is your greatest marketing tool because it is where you will point readers to in advertisements; many social media postings; book covers; biographies on author sites like Amazon, Goodreads, and Smashwords; contributing articles; guest blogs; and author interviews.

If you are an author who is serious about selling her work, you must have a professional website.

Websites should be visually appealing, practical, and designed for the user as well as for your business.

This should really go without saying: you must have a website if you want to reach out to the masses and build your author platform to its fullest potential. There are many website templates and hosting packages available. All you have to do is perform a simple search to find options.

There are some DIY sites to help you launch one yourself, and then there are the pros who can help you create a more sophisticated look. Be sure to contract someone who will create a site you can maintain on your own. There are some website consultants who will dazzle you with a beautiful site and charge you for each change you want to make later on. I made that mistake before, and it cost me dearly!

A good website consultant will work with you to create what you need, then train you on how you can maintain that going forward.

Websites serve many purposes – to welcome, invite, educate, sell, introduce, entice, or show off your appeal. I could go on for pages. The most important thing is that the website should reflect your brand and, on its simplest terms, be comprised of basic website necessities.

ONE-ON-ONE: THE POWER OF A WEBSITE

I sat down with my trusted web designer/developer, Micheal Petrulli from Brain Power Websites (www.BrainPowerWebsites.com), to get his expert opinion on website best practices and what authors should look for when considering a website company.

Q. Why does a writer need a website?

Michael: These days, your website may well be the first (or only) impression readers will see when they encounter your work. And while your books, blog posts, and pictures may be top-notch, if the website is subpar – slow, hard to navigate, out of date – potential visitors may click away and be done before they even have a chance to get to know anything about your work. A website is a reflection of your work, your professionalism, and your overall credibility.

Q. What is one of the biggest reasons website visitors click away from a website?

Michael: If readers are accessing your site via a mobile device, and your site is not mobile-friendly (mobile responsive), you're at a distinct disadvantage to keeping them on your site. A great majority of readers access the internet via their mobile devices. Forty percent of people have said they turned to a competitor's website after a bad mobile experience.

Q. What deserves prime real estate on a website?

Michael: You're a writer. You have books to sell. Access to purchase your books should be one of the most prominent features.

Q. How can a writer increase traffic to his/her site?

Michael: Curate content consistently. Google and other search engines give much more authority (and thus, visibility) to websites that are updated frequently. Your site will lose search engine rankings, and the resulting web visitors, if you are not consistently adding content relevant to your target market through blogging or the addition of new content. This brings me to an important point. Be sure to track web visits so you can accurately measure, analyze, and strategize your efforts for further success.

Q. What elements should be included on a homepage?

Michael: I recommend a "keep it simple" approach. Place too many items on your homepage or too much copy and visitors will become confused quickly. One of the biggest mistakes I've seen on websites is when it's littered with countless homepage buttons, way too many calls to action, footers that resemble file cabinets, and too much content getting in the way of clean and smooth navigation to central information.

Q. What elements should be featured on a website?

Michael: Visuals are a must. Images that catch the eye are important, as they break up the congestion of blocks of copy and free up the space. Also present information in a logical, sequential pattern. Start with a clear introduction to explain what you are about (i.e. Suzie Carr, novelist who admires the beauty of life's curves and enjoys writing books about some of the most interesting ones.), followed with the presentation (i.e. featured writing, blog postings), and finish with a conclusion/call to action (i.e. how to purchase a book, sign up for email newsletter, access to free writing course).

Q. How can a writer determine the most important, logical information to present?

Michael: Put yourself in your reader's shoes and ask *what's in it for me?* Ask this for everything on your home page and sales pages. The interests and/or needs of the reader should reflect to match your offering and content. My advice to clients when they are deciding on flow and navigation elements is:

Ask yourself, what do I want my website to do for me?

Be realistic and simple; remember that visitors' attention spans are fairly short when online.

Map out your thoughts by sketching it on paper.

Typically the pages to start with are: Home, About, Books, Blog, Media, and Contact.

Imagine your homepage as a tour guide.

The homepage is the place that will guide your readers where to go on your site for maximum benefit. The homepage will briefly mention enough about you and your work to get them interested enough to click on those important navigation links, hopefully inspiring them to take action.

Q. How can I ensure readers will find my website through a search?

Michael: Your website can be the most beautiful site in the world, but if it's not set up with Search Engine Optimization (SEO) in mind, readers may never find it through a search. Design and SEO go hand-in-hand. An effective website is one that is both beautiful and ranks well.

SEO should never be considered an add-on service. In order to work well, a site has to be found.

Q. What should a writer expect from a web design/development company?

Michael: A first step should be a consultation. The web consultant should ask you a lot of questions to get to know you and your work. To build a top-notch website requires careful thought and consideration.

This also gives you, as the client, a chance to become comfortable with the process.

After a consultation is performed, the next logical step you should expect is receiving a proposal that details the services and prices for the project. Once you accept a proposal, expect to pay a portion of the invoice upfront. Typically this is half of the invoice.

A quality developer will work closely with his clients once the project is kicked off. This is typically when the website framework is created, determining what pages will be included and how the site will flow.

At this stage, once framework is approved, development begins.

Personally speaking, once development begins, my team steps into the design process, using graphics/pictures provided by the client, as well as providing some if needed and keeping brand recognition in mind as well as the flow of the website.

This is where the site starts to take shape and is that time in the process where our client submits the content for the pages. Nobody knows a business like the client does, so I would always suggest the client to provide content.

Next is the exciting time when final reviews should be made, checking visuals and coding aspects, as well SEO setups. Then, it's launch time.

Q. Bottom line, what key factors should a writer look for in a web company?

Michael: Be sure they provide 24/7 service; website security (preventing malware and brute force attacks); hosting/domain options; a strong focus on functionality first, then cosmetic; research on competitors to provide an objective analysis prior to building your framework; a solid understanding of functionality (flow – navigation, clean, intuitive and smooth); onsite SEO services (these should be set up organically and built into site's foundation); and a mobile-friendly/responsive site.

I would recommend writers do their research before signing any contract. Get quotes from at least three providers and don't take the lowest or most expensive bid. Make sure you understand the conversation. I've seen a lot of people burned from not understanding the conversation and pretending to understand it out of fear of looking unintelligent because they couldn't understand the industry jargon. If a web professional is talking to you in industry jargon and not easy-to-understand language, walk away.

STEP 2: GAIN SOCIAL MEDIA RELEVANCE

I can't imagine what it must have been like to market a book before the advent of social media platforms like Twitter, Facebook, Google+, Instagram, Pinterest, Goodreads, and YouTube, and the arrival of hashtags.

Grateful doesn't even begin to describe my feelings about having something as robust as social media in my marketing mix. Sure, a time cost is associated with using these platforms, taking away from writing. Additionally, these platforms can cost money if you want to maximize your reach in a targeted manner. But not a penny has to be spent to get some serious mileage out of them as you build your readership.

With so many platforms, navigating them can become complex and overwhelming. To be on all, to the extent one would think you need to be to reap advantages, can easily tear you away from some serious writing time. Having a social media strategy is key! This will keep you from wasting valuable time online, and using your time most effectively when you are interacting.

So which social media platforms are best for writers? All the major ones.

Readers are everywhere, and we can't possibly reach them on any one or two platforms alone. Best practices suggest to connect with readers on as many platforms as possible. By doing this, you increase your reach and thus chances of having your readers see your post.

Let's delve into each and go through the benefits so you can decide for yourself on which ones you should focus the majority of your time.

I learned the following information via Social Media Examiner, Post Planner, and my own experiences as a marketing professional. I've taken the information learned and molded it to my specific needs, putting it to practice, testing out my own spin, and found success with it.

Twitter

Twitter is by far my favorite and most successful platform. According to my Google Analytic reports, Twitter brings on average at least three hundred unique visits to my website daily.

I opened a Twitter account a little over three years ago, and I have over seventeen thousand followers. I built up my Twitter following through simple interaction. I follow readers, writers, fellow health and wellness enthusiasts, animal lovers, and people who enjoy self-improvement. My content is focused around three areas on my blog and videos: life's curves, health and wellness, and writing. Most of the people I follow reciprocate the gesture. When someone follows me back, I begin the interaction immediately. I typically tweet to them or send a direct message, thanking them for the follow and beginning a dialogue exchange about any of the topics I mentioned above. I do not bring up my books in these personal exchanges unless someone asks me first. Remember, social media is a tool to help build relationships, not in-your-face sales.

That being said, eighty percent of my tweets are quotes, self-improvement tips, blog postings, videos I've created, pictures I've taken, silly thoughts that pop into my mind, and retweets of my followers. The other twenty percent are tweets where I include a snippet from a book review or excerpt and a link to the referenced book on Amazon. I am cognizant of not filling up my twitter feed with endless promo tweets. I don't want a potential follower to review my twitter feed and see nothing but links to my books. My goal on social media is to add value. That is my primary objective. I want what I post to be useful for people. If it's useful, they will share it, discuss it, and continue to trust in our exchange. A handful of promotional tweets thrown into a mix full of valued information is digestible to most followers, and many will take notice and click to purchase.

Top priority should always be to provide relevant, useful, valuable information on social media. Look at your tweets through your own lens. What kind of tweets do you retweet, favorite, and discuss? Would you interact with the tweets you're sending? If not, reevaluate and aim for value-driven content.

Twitter allows its users to post and receive messages to a network of contacts. You only have to post a tweet from your account, and the tweet is distributed to all your followers. It's a great tool to let others know what's happening.

Tweets are limited to 140 characters. That's it. If you want others to share your tweets (known as a retweet), consider shortening them to 100 characters so they can also add thought to the shared message.

Get Started

Twitter may look complicated at first glance, but it's really user-friendly. The first thing you want to do is set up your profile. This will include a username, short bio, profile photo, and a header image, all designed to show the world who you are.

Your @username, also known as your handle, is 15 characters or less. Make it memorable and representative of who you are so people will find you easily.

Next, write a short bio no longer than 160 characters that tells your story. Who are you? What do you write? What is your value? Be sure to include a trackable link to your website.

Your profile picture should be formatted to 400 x 400 pixels. This image will show up on every tweet and message, so choose one that represents you best.

Select a header image that showcases your personality. You can feature yourself or your books, and even include copy that highlights a promotion. This image should be 1500 x 500 pixels. When viewing on a mobile device, this image will be resized to a 2:1 aspect ratio.

Another neat Twitter feature is that you can pin a tweet to the top of your feed. This feature is great to gain maximum exposure for an important tweet. Simply click on the *more* option on the tweet you want to pin and select *pin to your profile page*.

Maximize Reach

Develop a strategy

Look at what others are tweeting. What do you like about what they are doing? What resonates with you? What would you be likely to share with your followers or interact with? A great tool for searching topics related to your own desires is to monitor conversations using

<u>search.twitter.com</u>. What are others doing? Test out their methods with your own followers.

Use the 80/20 principle

Twitter recommends that 80% of your tweets should focus on driving interactions with your followers, such as curated content, retweets, replies, and favorites. The other 20% should be a mix of direct offers or promotions that get followers to take actions, such as clicking on a link or making a purchase from your website.

Let your personality shine

To build rapport and relationships, you need to be true to your voice. People engage with wit, inspiration, helpful advice, and easy-going dialogue. This is your way of letting your readers get to know the real you.

Be consistent with your presence

Twitter moves fast, and if you're not posting several times daily, you're likely to get swallowed up in the masses. Set up your tweets in the morning. Schedule them to go out every hour or two. Make them relevant to your business (i.e. show off your personality, offer tips, link to blog posts and relevant articles, post quotes, say something funny, post specials, etc.)

Tell followers what to do

Add an action verb to your tweets: *check out this list, read this article, try this workout.*

Use images and videos

Nearly two-thirds of people are visual learners. Visual data is processed much faster than text by the brain, and adding videos to landing pages can increase conversions by nearly 90% (according to www.socialtimes.com). These are all good reasons to use images and videos in your mix.

Interact with your followers

Make it a two-way conversation by posing open-ended questions. To get people more engaged, ask for their suggestions. Ask questions that will strike up a lively discussion and hopefully pique your followers' curiosity to visit your website to read your blogs, learn more about your work, and get on your mailing list.

Thank your followers

Select a few each day and thank them for their support.

Retweet your followers

Each day, choose a few followers and retweet something of value. This shows your compassion, humanity, and eagerness to connect.

Additionally:

- Promote your @username everywhere
- Add a *follow* button to your website
- Get found with hashtags
- Follow a set number of new people daily
  - A word of caution, be sure not to follow too many people at once. Twitter doesn't like this and they may suspend your

account for short or long term. Be sure to read their terms and conditions. Based on their current terms and conditions, I choose to stay within the average of following ten to twenty people a day. Follow people who are relevant to your readership. Perhaps this is someone into fashion, someone who is a fan of dancing, or someone who enjoys the great outdoors. You can find them by visiting the pages of fashion or style magazines, reality television shows on dancing, and retail stores that cater to outdoor adventure, and then searching their *followers list*. Simply click on *follow* next to a person's name. If they follow you back, follow up with a thank you and an open-ended question. Also, be sure to visit their tweets and interact when possible.

Facebook

Facebook is a place where friends meet up, people from the past reconnect, communities gather, and information is shared. People flock to this virtual playground for entertainment and lively conversation. It's a place people share ideas, pictures, videos, and personal reflections.

Facebook provides several ways to connect by:

- Joining networks and browsing through the list of members to search for people you know
- Allowing Facebook to pull contacts from a web-based email account
- Using Facebook's search engine to look for a specific person

Once a profile is set up, Facebook offers fan pages. Much debate has circled around if a business (this includes writers!) should bother to create a fan page. Some writers have voiced that they prefer just using their profile to interact because they feel their posts are seen by more people. Fan page posts are not as readily seen organically, despite the fact that people have opted to see your posts. You have to pay to play with fan pages. It's a matter of fact and of doing business. So why would someone choose to pay if profiles allow a writer to be more readily seen organically?

Fan pages offer robust options not available on profiles. Unlike a profile, a fan page offers unique tools for businesses, brands, organizations, or celebrities, and is managed by admins who have profiles. Fan pages can be *liked* and have an unlimited number of fans. Pages come pre-installed with custom functionality, and many third-party apps are available for admins to add to their pages. Pages allow you to create custom apps to gather email leads for marketing outside of Facebook (THIS IS HUGE). Pages can run targeted ads to get traffic, emails, and likes. Pages can schedule future posts. Pages can access a large library of stats on posts, fans, demographics, etc.

Creating a fan page makes sense if your goals are aligned with the kind of outcomes listed above. If you want the option to advertise, target posts to a niche audience, analyze stats, use helpful apps, generate leads, and schedule posts ahead of time, then consider a fan page.

Get Started

- Upload a profile picture that is 180 x 180 pixels
- Upload a cover image that is 851 x 315 pixels
- Share photos that are 1200 x 1200 pixels
- Complete the information section to let friends or fans know more about you
- For a fan page: Add a featured video and customize tabs (i.e. Shop Now, Author App, Events, Videos, Goodreads, etc.)

Adopt Facebook Best Practices

Facebook is a place your readers hang out to interact with friends, watch fun videos, see beautiful images and funny quotes, play games, and connect with people of interest. It is not a place readers want to feel imposed upon with in-your-face promotions. So you'll want to tread carefully on this platform, especially if you are posting from a profile. Not only may readers get annoyed if they see repeated promotional-type posts, but they may report you. Get reported too much, and you could find yourself with a suspended account.

Personally, I post about 2-3 times a day, and usually post content that I believe is of value to my followers, page fans, and friends. These typically consist of fun photos of my furbabies, quotes I've created or am crediting to another artist, trending content, blog posts, and occasionally a thank you shout-out to someone who reviewed a book of mine. I also love asking questions. If you ask a question, make it incredibly easy for people to answer it.

Bottom line is that people don't like to be marketed to on Facebook. It is more of a relationship building environment.

One word of advice that can't be stressed enough is consistency. Be consistent and timely with your postings. If you must, schedule a post like you would a client in an appointment book. You must be present for engagement to work. Post a special, a note, a question, or fun piece of trivia once a week. The goal is to get people clicking, sharing, and liking your posts.

Ask yourself as you create posts:

- If I were scrolling my newsfeed and came across a similar post, would I *like* it, comment on it, or share it?
- If this is a photo post, is it relevant and empowering enough to cause someone to engage with it?
- Does this post offer something valuable in terms of tips, information, or entertainment?

Maximize Reach

- Use engaging copy, images and videos
- Add your website to each photo
- Use original photography whenever possible. If you use someone else's, be sure to obtain their permission
- Keep your posts between 100-250 characters to get more engagement; shorter, succinct posts are better received
- Create a conversation by asking for feedback, then responding to that feedback

- Offer special deals through your Facebook page to encourage more *likes*
- Create a conversation calendar – jot down a plan of what you'll say and when, creating a sense of consistency across the board (maybe one day you feature reader reviews, another writing tips, and another discussion points)
- Schedule your posts ahead of time to keep to your plan
- Use your website link in your posts to drive website traffic

Google Plus

A Google Plus account is based upon a Google profile and is made up of circles (networks). It's a collection of people with whom you want to connect. Your Google Plus account comes with three pre-defined circles: friends, family, and acquaintances, or you can customize your own circles. When you add someone new, you have the choice of which circle(s) to place him. This is not reciprocal. That person must add you to his circle for you to be connected in a two way interaction.

Circles let you share information with specific groups of people while excluding everyone else. You can also filter the information you read in your stream via circles. The main activity on Google Plus takes place in this stream. The stream is a lot like a Facebook wall – it's where you'll see status updates from the people you've chosen to follow in your circles.

In addition to circles, Google Plus includes a great interactive tool that allows you to video chat with up to ten people. It is called a Google Hangout. To participate in Hangouts, you'll need a webcam and microphone, and headphones to help reduce echoes.

Google Plus allows users to post their own content and share someone else's status update. If you want to share someone's update, simply click the *share* button to publish your friend's status update under your own stream. Google will attribute the shared post to your friend.

Get Started

If you already have a Google profile, getting started with Google Plus is easy. Your Google profile becomes your *about* page on Google Plus. Your profile photo will be pulled directly from your Google account. Be sure to upload a cover photo that is 2120 x 1192 pixels. As a side note, when sharing an image on Google Plus, the minimum size required is 250 x 250 pixels.

Maximize Reach

Initiate conversation

Post, respond to comments, and share other people's content.

Ask questions

This is a great way to understand your readers and to engage in interactive conversations.

Be grateful

A great way to build and retain loyalty is to be thankful. A simple thank you to a reader can go a long way. Simply tag the person you are thanking by using the @ or + symbol in front of the person's name.

Increase fun

Set up a poll asking about favorite books, characters, places to read, etc. People love answering polls!

Curate content

To increase your reach, you must offer rich content worthy of attention. Decide what that content is, curate it, and share it. Some of the most engaging content is often beautiful photos, inspiring quotes, interesting videos, and infographics. Check out news.me for curated ideas.

Stay fresh and consistent

Create a posting schedule and stick to it so followers know what to expect from you.

Stay personal

Stay true to your voice. Post fun things that give followers a glimpse of your personality, likes, and dislikes.

Instagram

Instagram is the popular picture app for smartphones that allows users to upload photos, apply easy-to-use filters, and personalize and share them. This is a fantastic marketing tool.

Instagram allows you to create an air of personal touch between you and your readers. You get to showcase your personality! Pictures can be goofy, serious, dramatic, lively, anything you want them to be. Readers get a behind-the-scenes peek, and this creates a personal touch that stretches beyond the scope of the pages in your books. Another neat feature is that Instagram is connected to Facebook and Twitter. So if you post a photo on Instagram, you can also choose to share it on multiple social media platforms.

Get Started

- Download the application to your smartphone
- Upload a profile picture; Instagram will resize it to 161 x 161 pixels
- Adjust your privacy settings to your liking

Maximize Reach

- Just as with all other social media programs, you have to stay active to continue to build and maintain your presence
- Use hashtags so people searching for your picture content can find you easily
- Interact with other people's photos and be responsive when others interact with your content

Pinterest

Think of Pinterest as a corkboard where you can pin visuals. Essentially, it is an online community where people can share interests and inspirations. Pinterest uses images instead of words. Users curate visually appealing items that are of interest to them. Every item pinned is linked back to its place of origin. So, if you pin a picture of your book cover, you can link it back to your website where readers can then access a way to purchase it.

Get Started

Pinterest offers two ways to sign up. Either with an email address (you'll be prompted to set up a short profile with this option) or via your Facebook or Twitter account.

Once signed up, Pinterest will show you a series of images and ask you to click on ones you find engaging. These images will help Pinterest set up your *following* page by categorizing areas of interest.

You can also connect with people you know by signing into your Gmail, Facebook or Yahoo account. Pinterest will populate a list of existing users you may know.

In addition to following people, you can follow categories, too. Perhaps you might want to follow a niche that resembles the genre of your book. For instance, if you write romance books, perhaps you might want to follow a category that caters to romance. Ultimately, for marketing purposes, you'll want to add images to your *boards* that connect you to your readership. Boards help you to organize ideas.

Image dimensions to keep in mind: Profile photo should be 600 x 600 pixels, board thumbnail 222 x 150 pixels, and pins 600 x infinite.

Maximize Reach

- Pinterest provides a *Pin it* button browser app that allows you to pin images from the far reaches of the web to your boards
  - When you find an image you like online, click the *Pin it* button and select the board you'd like to place it on. This is an awesome option because readers can click on the *Pin it* button on your website images and pin them to their boards for their followers to see. Any time an image is *pinned* like this, Pinterest automatically records the link to the item.
- Connect with other users by commenting or liking their pins
- Respond when someone comments on one of your pins

Goodreads

Goodreads is a free website for book lovers. Think of Goodreads as a gigantic library where readers shelve their books, select books to read, check out what others are reading, leave reviews, read reviews and ratings, and interact with other readers and writers in discussion groups and book clubs.

Get Started

To sign up on Goodreads, all you need to provide is a name, email, and password. Writers should sign up for the Author Program.

As a Goodreads Author, you'll want to add your books to your Goodreads Bookshelf. To add, simply supply your book's information to manually add it or use the add feature that searches for your book from several online book stores like Amazon, Kindle Store and anywhere you have your books for sale. Once signed up for the Author Program, readers can check out your photo, blog, books you've written, and books you've read.

Maximize Reach

Sync your blog

By syncing your blog with your Goodreads profile, you'll broaden your reach, thanks to Goodreads sending its members a weekly email with new blog posts from authors they like. As a member of the Author Program, you can promote events (i.e. online discussions and book releases) and invite your Goodreads friends to attend.

Do a book giveaway

Get people reading and talking about your book. Only print books are allowed to be in a giveaway, but you can participate in an unlimited amount of book giveaways. When a Goodreads member reviews a book it shows up on that member's newsfeed, providing word-of-mouth marketing.

Join groups and interact

Start interacting as a reader, not a writer. Once members get to know you in time, the moderators may be more receptive to hearing about your books and perhaps considering them for a discussion. Remember – relationship building is key. No one wants to be marketed to.

Create a Featured Author group

This offers writers the opportunity to interact with readers and create buzz about their books. By creating one, you are agreeing to answer questions about your books for a brief period. Goodreads will help promote the group using its word-of-mouth tools. Simply create a special group (i.e. Ask Suzie Carr or Suzie Carr hosts a Q&A). Categorize it as a *Goodreads Author* group. State what time range you will be available to answer questions – Goodreads recommends running your group for a single day and creating a single discussion topic (i.e. Ask me something!) to keep the discussion manageable in just a single thread. To start the thread, write a post welcoming everyone to your group and asking for questions.

YouTube

YouTube is currently the second largest search engine in the world. It is a creative way to get in front of a wide audience and educate, inform, and inspire. With a basic YouTube account you can upload videos; comment on other videos; create a favorites list, playlist, and personalized channel; subscribe to other channels; get subscribers to your channel; share videos; and interact with other users.

As a member, you can send private messages or make a comment for everyone to see through a user's personal channel. You can also comment on individual videos, unless the video's creator has turned off that feature.

Get Started

When you become a YouTube member, you are assigned a personal channel. Be sure to complete your profile information, including channel art that should be sized to 2560 x 1224 pixels. Your profile will be pulled from your Google account. You can also add a channel video to welcome people. This gives you the opportunity to introduce yourself, your books, and the types of videos people may come to expect on your channel. This is your virtual welcome mat!

Maximize Reach

Consistency

Stick to a consistent post schedule so you can stay engaged with your subscribers.

Curate videos from existing content

Create videos from blog posts turned into slides, book readings, book trailers, personal reflections, pets, a-day-in-the-life, daily thoughts, or anything that speaks to your readership. If you aren't sure how to shoot a video effectively, YouTube also has a section called the video toolbox, which features tips and tricks of video production. There are tutorials about lighting, video editing, camera angles, sound production and special effects.

Embed

Embed posted videos on your website and blog for extra reach.

Direct users

Encourage users to share your video and subscribe to your channel.

Suggest videos

Suggest additional videos of yours for users to watch.

Pay attention to Search Engine Optimization (SEO)

Complete the title, description and tags on all your uploaded videos for better searchability.

Use YouTube's tools

Use this tool: YouTube Creator Playbook – a comprehensive tutorial for everything YouTube has to offer.

Hashtags

The hashtag is likely the most popular means of categorizing content on social media. It makes your own content discoverable and allows you to find relevant content from other people and businesses. The hashtag also allows you to connect with and engage other social media users based on a common theme or interest.

Be specific

The goal should be high engagement. The more specific you can get with your hashtag, the more targeted your audience will be.

Be mindful of platform

Hashtags are used differently across platforms. Instagram hashtags, for example, are often more focused on description of the photo. With

Twitter, hashtags tend to be more focused on a topic of conversation. Before using hashtags, do research on the proper way to use them for that particular platform. Most platforms will have guides for hashtag selection.

Keep it short and sweet

Long hashtags won't be trending. Think searchable. You want people searching a hashtag to find your post.

Don't overuse

A general rule of thumb is to not have more hashtags than words. Too many hashtags just dilutes your message and makes you come across as chaotic and desperate to connect. Definitely use them across all social platforms, just don't overuse them.

STEP 3: CONTENT CURATION

I first started blogging back when I was writing my novel, *Inner Secrets*. Essentially, my blog was a personal journal written from the point of view of my main character Hope Steele. I would write journal entries talking about her experiences, opinions, streams of consciousness, and secrets, and this resulted in a wonderful following. Readers would comment on how much they could empathize with Hope's struggles and triumphs, and then they'd start to share their own stories.

Not only was I intimately getting to know my character, but this character was growing a fan base that wanted to hear her entire story. The result was an entire novel!

A few years later, long after publishing *Inner Secrets*, I ran out of ideas on what to blog about. I had no more *Inner Secret* entries to write because they all seemed anti-climactic after Hope's story came to a peaceful resolution. I decided my blog needed a whole new direction.

I consulted with a professional web developer and he created a nice, fresh website complete with a blog platform, lead generation email sign-up form, and all the bells and whistles a good author's website should have as discussed in the earlier section on websites.

I have a strong interest in health and wellness, in life's beautiful twists and turns, and in writing. So, why not blog about those topics that most interest me?

Flash forward to the present day, and I've created a blogging process that works for me. I blog every other week, alternating between the three topics listed in the previous paragraph. Not only do I get to research, learn, and share valuable information, but I also get to interact with people, expand my reach, and get people visiting my website.

The reason I find such success on platforms like Twitter is because of the content I've created. I don't just write a blog post, post it for a day or two, then let it die in my archives. I continue to share that post over and over again and meet new readers as a result.

Content curation is your biggest traffic generator. If you want to reach readers, you need to curate content, and a blog is the home base for your content.

Why Blog?

Build contacts

Each website visitor is a potential reader. Capture this visitor's email and you can communicate with her on a regular basis.

Out of sight, out of mind

You want to be on the minds of readers. When someone is searching for a new book to read on the weekend, you want them to remember your name. If they never hear from you, they may forget you. Give readers a valuable reason to come back time and again.

Form a trusting bond

Ongoing communication can build trust over time, especially when you offer them information that is of value.

Create an Ideal Blog

- Keep your headline under six words (recommended tool to determine a headline's effectiveness: www.aminstitute.com/headline
- Hook readers with a great anecdotal opening paragraph
- Use a featured image
- Use subheads for scanning

- Keep content to the sweet-spot of 1,500 words
- Use a friendly interface like Wordpress; it offers easy-to-use tools, valuable plug-ins, opt-in subscriber form, and lots of templates
- Be sure to link back to other pages on your site
- Encourage comments and engage with those who take the time to leave one

Curate Different Types of Content

Adding value-driven information to your blog posts can help increase readership. Here are some examples of additional resources to provide in your blog postings, or even as incentives to sign up for your blog through email.

- How-to's
- Giveaways
- Videos
- Surveys
- Guides
- Infographics
- Exclusive interviews with other authors
- Sneak peeks into a work-in-progress
- Polls
- Podcasts
- Photos (DEFINITELY PHOTOS)

ONE-ON-ONE – BLOGGING

I sat down with Amit Verma, C.E.O & Founder @ModernLifeTimes & @ModernLifeBlogs and asked for his expert advice on how to be successful as a blogger.

Q. Why should a writer consider a blog or newsletter?
Amit: If you are a writer, it's critical that you own a blog. This is because your main source of writing success is your website, and so your responsibility is to make it up-to-date with information that not only attracts visitors, but also helps drive traffic to your site. Blogging is the perfect option for this because every blog post written is also indexed on search engines like Google, Yahoo or Bing. Essentially, every post is a new opportunity to generate new leads.

Q. What are the essentials a writer should include in a blog/newsletter?
Amit: There are many things that a writer should consider. Let's check them out one by one:

Design

The most important essential element of a blog is your website design. If your website design is attractive and user friendly, then this helps gain returning visitors and more traffic to your blog. If you're a do-it-yourselfer, conduct some research on website templates that match your blogging categories. If you prefer to hire a professional, look for one who can help design it around your established brand presence on the web. Note: Use responsive designs so your blog and your email can be read by all readers no matter what device they are using it.

Plugins

WordPress is the best tool for hosting your website/blog because of their vast array of plugins that help make your website more user-friendly. These plugins provide you with the ability to generate leads. WordPress requires a good host, though, so always use a reliable web hosting company like Hostgator, BlueHost, or Godaddy. Use VexxHost Cloud Sites if you want to host your website on cloud servers.

Social networks

Engaging with your audience is a win-win deal. Social media sites like Twitter and Facebook not only help your website get traffic, but also help you in connecting with readers from all over the world. You can interact with your followers by doing #hashtag activities on Twitter or running a contest on a Facebook page, for example. Support other bloggers by sharing their blog posts. This will help build relationships and widen your reach.

Comments

Ensure you have a comments feature. This is a fun way to get interaction on your site. To encourage comments, ask a question at the end of every blog post. Something as simple as *what do you think* or *do you have a view to share* are great ways to invite readers to join in a conversation.

Q. Are there best practices for blogging?

Amit: Getting results requires dedicated work. So in blogging, to enjoy successful outcomes, you'll have to be willing to put in the hard work. Let's check out the best practices of blogging that you can implement to get better results:

Planning

Before starting anything, you should plan. Set a blogging goal by creating a calendar. Decide what dates and topics you will blog about and then stick to it. The better you plan, the more success you are bound to have.

Writing techniques

Try writing your headline first, then taking a bird's-eye view approach of your content. Does it flow logically? Does it make a point? Is there continuity in the presentation? Ultimately, if you are doing it right, your web pages and site will retain and attract more visitors.

Readers/Audience

Know your audience and write about topics that they will enjoy. Write content that will entertain them so they share your content, and then you get more visitors. Write engaging titles to pique their interest. If your blog or newsletter entertains your audience, then loyalty of readership will increase.

Images

Images make content more interesting and play a vital role in attracting the wide audience. Search for engaging images to add to your posts that not only beautify it, but also give a bold impression to your blog post.

Q. How can a writer be most successful as a blogger? Any tips for newbies?

Amit: Blogging, although rewarding on many levels, is not an easy job. To be successful with it, you have to do the work. It takes time and patience to build a loyal readership. If you are new to blogging, then here are a few tips to make your journey somewhat easier:

Unique articles

Produce great content consistently. Aim to write compelling posts about things you care about and others do, too. If you enjoy writing your posts, your passion will come through. Readers who enjoy your content may share it with others or add a link to your post on their website. This, of course, offers great traffic-building advantages.

Engage

Interact with other bloggers in your niche through commenting on their blogs or via social media. By communicating in this way, you will learn from them and grow a strong, supportive network.

Guest post

A great way to build awareness of your blog and website is to participate in guest blogging on other sites. Look into guest blogging on sites that are related and similar to yours. Guest posting on high traffic and high PR blogs is highly beneficial, as it will give you more exposure and quality back links.

Community

Present your blog in such a way that when new visitors come to it, they will feel a sense of community and want to become a part of it. Use plugins like BuddyPress, bbPress or any other membership plugins that transform your website into a social community.

Q. Is there any other piece of advice you have to offer aspiring writers from a blogging/social media perspective?

Amit: If you want to be a blogger, then always be seeking content to help you engage with your audience to keep them visiting your site regularly.

Blogging is not a simple task and requires hard work and patience before you may reap success. My advice is as follows:

- **Support** everyone and listen to your heart
- **Listen** to what your audience is talking about and try to understand their likes/interests
- **Start conversations** about your work, website, or blog; this is most important for social media success
- **Sharing is caring**; always look for opportunities to share others' content
- **Take the time** to interact, give back, and use replies and retweets; Be sure to comment on blogs in the most helpful ways possible

STEP 4: DISTRIBUTION & LEAD GENERATION

Curating a list of leads is imperative if you want keep in touch on a regular basis with your readership. Email is still the most reliable form of communication.

It took me many years to learn this.

When I first starting blogging about *Inner Secrets*, I used Google Blogger. It worked at the time, but one thing I had never considered in those early years was that Blogger didn't offer a way to collect emails should I ever want to get in touch with those following my blog.

The lightbulb to collect emails came to me one day when a friend's Twitter account was suspended indefinitely because he broke the rules in their terms and conditions over something to do with repeated posts. At the time, Twitter was my go-to for spreading the word about my books, upcoming releases, and new blog posts. I had roughly seven thousand followers back then, and I panicked thinking I could lose contact with all of them if I made a stupid mistake, too. And how many of those seven thousand followers really saw my news if I tweeted something out? Twitter is random. It is great for spreading the word to the masses, but my goal was to have a more intimate one-on-one communication pathway with my readers. That's when it hit me: *I need to manage my communications better.*

I have a lead generation capture tool on my site from MailChimp. Visitors can opt to receive news, blog postings, and communications from me. At any time, if they choose, they can unsubscribe from this list. Any reputable HTML service provider will offer subscriber widgets to correctly generate permission-based lists, provide easy-to-manage opt-outs, and allow you to track the success of each HTML email campaign. Keep your subscriber form simple, and be sure to thank each new subscriber and communicate your respect for his or her privacy.

With a targeted email list, you will have access to a captive audience who has granted you permission to send them information electronically.

Companies like MailChimp and Constant Contact make it super easy to create compelling, visually-appealing emails that are mobile friendly. Many of these service providers offer templates that make it easy to upload images and text. I personally use and love MailChimp. Their site is easy to use, robust, and affordable. I am able to easily set up forms to capture emails, create professional emails, and also set up auto-responder emails that I use with my Writer's Insights Video Series and free audio book, *Inner Secrets*.

CHAPTER INSIGHTS

- View a website as your home base
- Hire a professional if you don't know how to create a compelling site
- Be sure your site is mobile-friendly and optimized
- Use several social media platforms to interact with readers
- Provide useful, valuable information across several social media outlets
- Develop a schedule for posts to stay consistent
- Consider a Facebook fan page if you want robust marketing options
- Enhance interaction with readers via the Goodreads Author Program
- Use hashtags to make content more discoverable
- Curate content consistently to drive traffic to your website
- Use permission-based lead generation techniques

TO SUM IT UP

I'll say it again, I can't think of a better way to enjoy life than through the written word. And if you feel the same, I am thrilled for you. I hope you feel the same way I do about writing. I love how it takes me to levels outside routine, pushes me far beyond the status quo, and coaxes me into the creative arms of an unexplored world just brimming with possibilities to be discovered.

My wish for you is that you've got a real sense of passion that will sweep you up into the adventure of a lifetime. If you can tap into passionate emotions and really go for this endeavor, because it's who you are and it's in your core, then you will go far and readers will find you.

Success really comes down to setting goals that are personally rewarding and emotionally strong, to planning and thinking things through on a strategic level, to focusing and refocusing on tactics until they feel right, to measuring your actions and ensuring you're being as effective as you can, and mostly, it boils down to having a deep love and passion for being a part of something greater than yourself.

Now roll up your sleeves. You have a book to write!

Resources

Blogging sites to check out: modernlifetimes.com and modernlifeblogs.com

Book cover designer: www.germz808.com

Book design tool: www.diybookcovers.com

Daily email with curated stuff: news.me

Editing services: www.twintweaksediting.com

Facebook news: www.facebook.com/business/news | newsroom.fb.com/

Facebook post ideas: www.postplanner.com

Headline analyzer tool: www.aminstitute.com/headline

Hosting services: www.godaddy.com | www.hostgator.com

HTML email templates: www.mailchimp.com | www.constantcontact.com

Image tool: www.canva.com | www.picmonkey.com

Life coach training: www.tailoredtrainingsolutions.com

Keywords and SEO information: adwords.google.com

Popular hashtags and a bunch of analytical tools: twitonomy.com

Social media experts: www.socialmediaexaminer.com

Twitter applications: www.tweetdeck.com | www.hootsuite.com

Website consultants, templates, hosting packages: www.brainpowerwebsites.com

ABOUT THE AUTHOR

Suzie Carr is a novelist, publishing company owner, philanthropist, marketing professional, and avid blogger at www.curveswelcome.com.

Whether it's writing about love, inspiring new authors, advocating for LGBT equality and animal welfare or blogging about community awareness, positive living, taking action and inspiration... Suzie remains passionate in her beliefs!

She believes that love is love and that love knows no gender. She also believes in the power of community and fostering a welcoming place where everyone feels connected and their voices are equal, valued and appreciated.

With nine bestsellers on Amazon Kindle, Suzie continues to write about the beauty of love to the rave reviews of her growing fans, loyal followers and fellow authors.

NOTE FROM THE AUTHOR

As with all of my books, I enjoy giving a portion of proceeds back to the community by donating to the NOH8 Campaign www.noh8campaign.com and Hearts United for Animals www.hua.org. Thank you for being a part of this special contribution.

A SPECIAL REQUEST

If you found this book to be helpful, I'd be so grateful for your honest review of it. Just a sentence or two saying what you found helpful about *Writer's Insights* will help others discover it and help me to serve you better with future books!
(www.amazon.com/author/suziecarr)

Index

www.ingramcontent.com/pod-product-compliance
Lightning Source LLC
Chambersburg PA
CBHW022108280326
41933CB00007B/300